BUILDING BRIDGES
TOGETHER

BUILDING BRIDGES
TOGETHER

By Fred & Val Bennett

BUILDING BRIDGES TOGETHER

First Printing 2009. Building Bridges Together. Main Street Books.
ISBN 978-0-9801152-3-9

Published by Revival Nation Publishing
Print Edition ISBN 978-1-926625-28-7
eBook Edition ISBN 978-1-926625-29-4

Printed in the United States of America

Revival Nation Publishing
Ontario • CANADA

P.O. Box 30001
RPO Eastland Plaza
Sarnia, Ontario
N7T 0A7

www.RevivalNationPublishing.com

DEDICATION

Blessed are all who fear the Lord, who walk in his ways.
You will eat the fruit of your labor;
Blessings and prosperity will be yours.
Your wife will be like a fruitful vine within your house'
Your sons will be like olive shoots around your table.
Thus is the man blessed who fears the Lord.
May the Lord bless you from Zion all the days of your life;
May you see prosperity of Jerusalem,
And may you live to see your children's children.
Peace be upon Jerusalem.
Psalm 128 NIV

This book is dedicated to our:

son Chris Bennett and his wife Becky Mediwake Bennett,

daughter Denise Bennett Horn and her husband Jeremy Horn,

grandchildren: Maia, Levi and Claire Bennett,

Judah and Liam Horn.

TABLE OF CONTENTS

INTRODUCTION

So, go now and write all this down.
Put it in a book
So that the record will be there
to instruct the coming generations,

Isa 30:8

My first book 'Christ The Rock Metro Church, Our Story' was mainly the history of our lives on how the Lord found us, called us, and used us to pioneer this local church while crossing many bridges. In fact, the story ended in October of 2002 with the grand opening of our new 3000 seat Worship Center.

Our family at that time consisted of our son Chris and his wife Becky, along with their new born daughter, our first granddaughter, Maia, and our daughter Denise. Since then, our family has expanded. Chris and Becky have given us our second and third grandchildren, Levi and Claire. Our daughter, Denise, married Jeremy Horn, and they have blessed us with two boys, Judah and Liam. Our quiver is full! All of these added blessings have truly enlarged and enriched our family and caused us great joy. We can add to our repertoire of responsibilities, that of babysitting, in order to allow our children to function in the ministry God has called them to. He knew what He was doing in giving grandchildren at our seasoned age because they keep us smiling and our minds off of the drama of life. This phase of life is exhilarating and exhausting at the same time. As the saying goes, we anxiously await their arrival but are always glad to see the tail lights of their vehicles depart. They are our sleeping pills! Only a grandma and a papaw would understand that statement. Grandchildren truly are a heritage from God. Proverbs 17:6a NIV *Children's children are a crown to the aged,*

The ministry went through change and transition not long after entering 'the big house', the 3000 seat worship center. Some of the people who were with us in leadership have moved on to new 'Macedonian Callings' which made room for the next generation to move up. Denise and Jeremy were appointed Student Ministry Pastors after having served as Associates. And they became the Praise and Worship Leaders and overseers of the College and Career age group. Jeremy also released his first CD, 'Atmosphere', on the Grove label. Becky was named Children's Pastor and Chris was installed as Senior Pastor of Christ The Rock Church. What a picture of the generational blessing! A bridge to the next generation! To God be the glory! He is the Father of Abraham, Isaac, and Jacob who became Israel. If God can pass the baton to the third generation, He can get it to a thousand. Our children are every parent's dream. They are such an asset and blessing to us personally and to the ministry. They have in their heart to continue in order to leave an inheritance to their children. The bridge continues.

Join us as we narrate phase two of our story. God is a God who is always on the move, transforming our lives because His ultimate goal is to have an invisible building He can dwell in that will be an influence on the culture. His message never changes because it is foundational, but His methods do in order to be relevant. He wants us to be an aroma that will draw people to Him so that His Kingdom can expand.

Yes, we have crossed many bridges. There have been times when the ministry has been exhilarating and at other times heart wrenching. All in all, God is Sovereign and He sustains us in all circumstances because He sees the big picture. Our prayer is that you will be encouraged, and that you will receive an impartation of what it means to truly serve God with all of your heart. We have celebrated over 40 years of marriage and 30 years of being Pastors. We are far from perfect but we do have the Perfect One abiding in us, motivating and directing us to cross still another bridge in our lives. So, our invitation is to come, walk with us as we build bridges together!

CHAPTER 1

THE FORTY YEAR SPAN
BUILDING A BRIDGE

*Do you see what this means —
all these pioneers who blazed the way,
all these veterans cheering us on?
It means we'd better get on with it.
Strip down, start running — and never quit!*

Hebrews 12:1

1967

was an interesting year. It was the year, Valerie Michaud and I met. We were married the following year, so now we've been together for over 40 years. We have been through much and survived, even thrived to the glory of God. In the Bible a 40 year span is called a generation and it is interesting to note how God works in 40 year increments. Certainly people then and now lived longer than 40 years, but 40 years seems to be the span of time most people remain active, productive and open to change.

I like the use of the word "span" in regards to this time frame because it is also another name for a bridge. At the beginning of August, 2007, the I-35W bridge that connected the twin cities of Minneapolis and St. Paul, Minnesota, collapsed into the Mississippi River. That bridge was built in 1967 and collapsed 40 years later. It was finally ruled that this huge span failed because of "structural deficiencies".

Not coincidentally, the mission declaration of our ministry and the title of this book is "Building Bridges Together". Our relationship started with us crossing the international bridge over the St. John River between Maine and New Brunswick, Canada, the night we met. And from the very beginning of our ministry 30 years ago we've been building and crossing bridges wherever there was a divide or a gap. We've built bridges between generations, denominations, races, nations, and between the church and the un-churched. But after 40 years, we began asking the Lord if it was time for us to do something else?

The answer to our query about changing our mission statement came with a sudden resounding boom! We were reminded of just how important it is to build and maintain bridges that last. When that bridge collapsed into the Mississippi River in Minnesota, witnesses said, 'it suddenly shook and just fell into the river'. Tragically, several people died and many were injured as the traffic was bumper to bumper during rush hour.

It appears that structural deficiencies went unnoticed because the span did not receive proper inspections and maintenance. The bridge connections were dirty, corroded and weakened. The inspection hole was just big enough for a man's head but the space was infested with birds and rats. Isn't that what happens to us in our relationships? Some things are just too ugly and scary to stick our heads into! And with the passing of time, although things look fine superficially, yet underneath, hidden away, are corroded and weakened connections!

If we are going to be a part of what I call the 'Crossover Generation', numbered among those who are still actively engaged in the expansion of the kingdom of God, then we need to inspect and maintain our important connecting relationships. This is especially true of our marriages. Just because a relationship has been around for a long time is no guarantee that it will continue.

Today we find ourselves at the end of a 40 year span, and the beginning of another. We are standing on the threshold of something new and exciting in the kingdom of God. Some things like old leaders, the old economy, the old politics, and even the old church are shaking and failing because of weak connections. In other words, the degree of disorder in a system will eventually destroy it. Old things will pass away and new things will come. Many of our old ways cannot continue if we are going to be the generation God has called us to be.

CHAPTER 2

THE MADAWASKA BRIDGE
DESTINY

I know what I'm doing. I have it all planned out —
plans to take care of you, not abandon you,
plans to give you the future you hope for.

Jeremiah 29:11

Fred and I come from totally divergent backgrounds. He is an American southern boy, born and reared in Memphis, Tennessee, Elvis Presley's home town. He is the eldest of four children with a strong Protestant work ethic background. I was born and reared in New Brunswick, Canada, the eldest of eight children by a British mother, a WWII war bride and a French Canadian father. My religious background was Catholic. We were twenty years old when we met and just beginning our careers. He was an airman serving in the United States Air Force and I was a seventh grade public school teacher.

The first bridge we crossed was the Madawaska Bridge which spans the Saint John River that acts as a boundary for the province of New Brunswick, Canada and the state of Maine, USA. Fred and I met in Madawaska Maine in the Fall of 1967. This era was called the 'Age of Aquarius', the hippy movement was in full bloom, free love was prevalent, getting high on drugs was popular, and rebellion against all authority was in vogue. In the midst of all of this, there was an unpopular war with an unpopular president. This was the backdrop for our encounter over forty years ago.

Fred's first assignment after basic training and technical school, was Loring Air Force Base located in the most northern part of Maine near Caribou, usually the coldest place in the US on weather map reports. What a shock for a southerner! I was living not far from the Madawaska International Bridge just on the outskirts of Edmundston, New Brunswick, in a village called Iroquois. Now that I am looking in the rear view mirror at our lives, this was truly the hand of God orchestrating our lives together. It was destiny and some would say fate that we should meet. We both happened to be at the same club that particular evening. What is interesting about this particular night was that I had declined any invitation to dance. Then lo and behold, Fred Bennett asks and I accept. Why? It is a mystery to me. He told me afterwards that he had been watching me and had a ready answer for me when I refused him. I surprised him and myself by accepting. I thought he was a student at a local university. He did not appear to be or act like the 'fly boys', a derogatory term for the military. He was a gentleman and very handsome! I was very surprised to find out he was an airman but that did not seem to matter then.

He asked if he could take me home and I accepted. It was always a 'no no' for me because I came with several of my girl friends and we always left as a group. This was different! He had the cutest little red sports car, an MG. It would not start that particular night because of the cold so he asked me to 'pop the clutch' because this car did not have an automatic transmission. I had no idea what he was talking about because I did not own a car or even know how to drive. Canadians did not own cars like the Americans did at that time. As soon as Americans turn 16 years of age, they get their driver's license and buy a car, and then have to have a job all through high school in order to pay the note, purchase the gas and the insurance. We Canadians took the bus, walked, or rode bikes. That was the way it was. Fred showed me how to 'pop the clutch' and we drove across the Madawaska Bridge for the first time together.

Here is a prophetic picture of an American and Canadian beginning to build a bridge together. We must have crossed that bridge hundreds of times. Sometimes several times a day! There was no drama in those days. No passports were required because the customs agents got to know us due to our frequent crossings so they would just wave us by. This was long before 9/11 (the Twin Tower tragedy on September 11, 2001in New York City), the age of terrorism we now live in where fear seems to permeate every area of life.

From that moment on, we saw each other almost every night for the next nine months. Nine represents birthing and fruitfulness in the Bible! I believe God was preparing us for our future together. In this case, a marriage and all that it would entail, of which we had little knowledge. Then unexpectedly, Fred received orders to go on a temporary assignment for four months on the island of Guam so we decided to get hitched because we did not want to lose each other. We were in love. We had one week to prepare so I made my dress and he bought a suit with his last pay check. We had no money for an elaborate celebration or reception. We married in St. Basile Catholic Church with our Parish Priest officiating. Fred's best man was a Jew and my sister Pat was my maid of honor. Fred was an American and I a Canadian. He was Methodist and I Catholic. We were in the process of building a bridge together even in this ceremony. After a three day honeymoon at the Loring Motel near the Base, Fred left for his tour of duty and I continued to live with my family until his return.

We had an interesting honeymoon! Before Fred departed, he helped me write my Political Science term paper because he has a better understanding of anything having to do with politics. I was attending St. Louis College at the time in order to finish my BA in education. I had attended Teachers College in Fredericton for two years and obtained a Teachers License. I was hired as a 7th grade teacher at Sacred Heart School in Edmundston, located on the street behind where my grandmother lived. She used to tell me when I was a little girl that I would be teaching at that school and have lunch with her every day. And so it was! She used to share stories with me about what life was like when she taught in a one room school building. Interesting! I believe that seed was passed along to me. Teachers seem to crop up in the third generation in my family because my granddaughter, Maia, says she is going to be a teacher when she grows up. It is almost scary because I see myself in her!

Fred came back after his stint in Guam and we set up our first apartment, just across the Madawaska Bridge in the town named after the bridge. He drove to the Base every day, a distance of about 60 miles, and I crossed the bridge every day to go to my teaching job at the local school. Eight months later Fred received new orders to go to Thailand for a year. This was very bad news for us because we were just beginning to adjust to our new roles as husband and wife. We knew there was that possibility that he could be shipped out since he was a member of the Strategic Air Command branch and airmen were often sent on temporary duty somewhere in the world. At that time the United States was at war with Vietnam. We had been hoping that it would not come to this, that he would spend the rest of his time in Maine, and then once he was discharged we would move back to Canada. Fred was and has always been enthralled with Canada. To this day, he calls it home when he talks about my home town. Canada was imprinted in his heart over forty years ago.

When the assignment came, we even contemplated evading this tour of duty by just crossing the bridge into Canada and staying there. So many Americans had already avoided the draft and others had deserted in order not to go to Vietnam. This assignment was going to be a difficult one. Being apart for a whole year! Could our marriage survive? But our consciences would not allow us to give into our emotions, and being a deserter did not fit our ethos. We were both reared to always do the right and just thing. So he obeyed his orders and was sent to Thailand. However, he was able to come home for a few days at Christmas which was a little over halfway through his tour of duty. It was better than nothing and we dreamed of the time when he would return home to Maine to fulfill the last stretch of his enlistment and move to Canada which was his heart's desire. So he crossed the Asian bridge and lived and worked on B-52 bombers in Thailand for a whole year. We wrote each other everyday. I got involved in all kinds of activities with people to pass the time and compensate for the loneliness I was feeling. A sense of community helps people through difficult times. Isolation is not the way to go when times are tough.

We continued to dream about our life together in Canada. We lived and breathed it. We were so focused on our future that we merely existed in the present at that time. That is no way to live! However, it was a good motivating force to have a plan in place because it compelled us to keep on keeping on as the saying goes. I once heard Joyce Meyer, a Bible teacher, say: "We should enjoy where we are on the way to where we are going". We even began purchasing big items for our 'future house in Canada' because they were much cheaper in the US even though the American dollar was worth less than the Canadian dollar at that time. Hard to believe! We were preparing to cross the Madawaska bridge and resume our lives in Canada. We were in process of building a bridge together. We were so excited because it gave us something to hold on to. Everyone needs a future because it gives form and focus to strive for a better life. The Bible tells us that without a vision or purpose, people have no hope.

Habakkuk 2:3 NKJV *For the vision is yet for an appointed time; But at the end it will speak, and it will not lie. Though it tarries, wait for it; Because it will surely come, It will not tarry.*

CHAPTER 3

THE MILITARY BRIDGE
THE DETOUR

"Don't force me to leave you; don't make me go home.
Where you go, I go; and where you live, I'll live.
Your people are my people,
your God is my god

Ruth 1:16

Fred came back from his tour of duty to Thailand and to our utter amazement, his new assignment was Westover Air Base in Chicopee Massachusetts. That meant we were going to spend the last nine months of his military duty there before being discharged from the Air Force. This unexpected turn of events threw us into a quandary! We were so sure that he would finish out his enlistment at Loring Air Force Base in Maine that it never even crossed our minds that we might have to relocate.

Because this new assignment interfered with our plans, we contemplated on whether or not I should stay in Canada till he was finished with his commitment to the military which meant another nine months apart. We had been apart sixteen months out of two years of marriage. This was no way for a married couple to live or for a marriage to survive. We decided the best thing was to relocate together. In the midst of this unforeseen plan unfolding before us, we felt excitement for the unknown. It was like living on the edge. We have never been conventional people. It seems like we are always going against the status quo in our lives. Looking back we realized God was in control preparing us for our future. God uses all of our life experiences to propel us into our destinies.

So I resigned from my teaching position which I loved dearly and accompanied my husband to Massachusetts. I felt like Ruth 1:16 when she said: *"Don't force me to leave you; don't make me go home. Where you go, I go; and where you live, I live. Your people shall be my people..."*
We hooked up a U-Haul trailer to our car with all of our earthly possessions which wasn't much and headed south. It was a nine hour drive from Madawaska to Chicopee. We still toyed with the idea that come March upon completion of his tour of duty, we would return to Canada

and I would resume my teaching career. The only work I found in Massachusetts was that of a saleswoman in a local department store selling cameras and the paraphernalia that goes with this hobby. It was fun and yet my pride was wounded because being a teacher was my identity. I rationalized that this was just a temporary position and that as soon as this stint was fulfilled, and Fred was discharged from the military, we would be heading back to Canada and I would resume my teaching career.

Our time in Massachusetts was an extremely lonely one. There was nothing familiar about this place. We dared not make new friends because we knew our time there was temporary. We had already experienced a severing of ties and everything familiar when we left the State of Maine, and the idea of doing it again was too painful. I was also very homesick and we could not afford to call home frequently. Inexpensive cell phone rates were not yet invented or developed. Needless to say, our social life was a big fat zero! We could not afford to go out much so we bought a ping-pong table that served as our entertainment. We had each other and that was enough. We were enjoying being together again and adjusting to married life. It was like our third honeymoon, the second being his return from Guam!

This time however, we were hoping there would be no more interruptions from the military. Fred had nine months left before being discharged. This situation bred insecurity and fear in our relationship because we were always dreading orders from the military. We would get to the place in our marriage where we would find comfort and fulfillment with each other and then the military would interrupt our relationship by sending Fred overseas. We would have to start all over again being a couple when he returned. They controlled us and we resented it. We felt like we were merely existing, feeling as though we were in limbo. We were waiting impatiently for this season to be over so that we could exit the military and enter a normal civilian life. This place was truly a detour on our way to whatever bridge we were going to build together!

Besides learning to become one in our marriage and overcoming the stresses of the military, I was trying to adapt to the American way of life. For example, grocery shopping was a task which took forever because I did not recognize any of the items we needed due to the difference in packaging and manufactures. I also felt isolated where language was concerned because of the barriers in pronunciation, use of acronyms and slang expressions which were so difficult for me to comprehend. One would not think that American English and Canadian English would be that different due to the close proximity of both countries, but they are! There were days when I would open my mouth and begin to speak French only to realize where I was. It was so strange and I really felt like a foreigner.

The northern part of the state of Maine was not at all dissimilar to Canada. People looked alike, dressed alike and even spoke some form of French. The only distinguishing mark was the bridge that separated our nations or I should say joined them. By moving further away from the border, I was not only crossing a physical bridge but a philosophical one, from the Canadian mindset to the American one. That sounds easier said than done! Americans in general tend to be very secure in who they are and might even appear to be arrogant due to the fact that the US is the most powerful nation on the planet; whereas we Canadians tend to fear living in their shadow while wanting to maintain our distinction and tend to be a more humble people as a whole. Americans think big while we think little. That is why Canada is much more accepted around the world. These are simply my observations and not intended to offend.

So we continued dreaming and planning, scheming and plotting our return to Canada come March 1971 upon Fred's discharge from the military. I look back on this period of our lives and see the hand of God preparing us for a future move even further away from Canada. Had we known God and had a relationship with Him, life would have been easier to accept because we would have known that He sees the big picture and we could have trusted Him in ordering our steps. He still did only we were not aware of it. We could have been praying and receiving His peace instead of being in such turmoil and fear over the future and the unforeseen change of events. I am glad He never lets us know ahead of time what He is doing otherwise we would freak out. We did not know it but He was teaching us to cross the familiar bridge to the unfamiliar one. It was the beginning of many crossings we were going to experience over the years to come in order to build new ones.

A funny thing happened! Another unforeseen event! Again our plans had gone awry! Fred got an early discharge in January of 1971 in order to resume his education at the University of Memphis where he had begun before entering the military. No door opened for us to return to Canada! Only Memphis Tennessee! We came to the conclusion that going back to Canada had been a pipe dream all along, that we had simply deceived ourselves. So we decided to drive home for Christmas right before his discharge because we did not know when we would be back. We ended up driving in a blizzard at a snail's pace on route 1 because the turnpike had been closed. It took 24 hours to get home instead of the nine. Upon arrival, we said 'Merry Christmas', had our festive dinner by ourselves, slept a few hours, and got back in the car and returned to Massachusetts. It was like our last effort to spend time in Canada was ruined. We were so disappointed! What a way to leave Canada!

It was not meant to be so we made preparations to move to Memphis. Once again we got a U-Haul trailer packed with all of our worldly possessions and headed further south leaving behind us winter with its mountains of snow and sub-zero temperatures. 'Déjà-vu' as they would say in French! At least this time, we were going to where Fred had been born and raised, and his family resided there which was a plus for us because it meant we would not be alone. We crossed the bridge from military life and began to build one to civilian life! What a relief!

Memphis is the city where Martin Luther King Jr. had been assassinated in 1968, a city where racial tensions still exist to this day. This is the city God was calling us to because He had plans for us. We didn't have a clue and still did not have a relationship with Him yet. In a sense we were going to a place in faith like Abraham in the Bible.

Genesis 12:1 TLB *Leave your own country behind you, and your own people, and go to the land I will guide you to.*

For a young girl who had lived all of her life in the small community of Iroquois just outside the city of Edmundston, New Brunswick (except for two years in Fredericton while attending Teachers College) going to

Memphis Tennessee sounded so exciting and romantic. After all, this is where Elvis Presley lived! This is the city Johnny Rivers sang about!

Good bye North! Hello South! Here I come to the land of Dixie!

CHAPTER 4

THE MEMPHIS-ARKANSAS BRIDGE
PREPARATION

Many are the plans in a man's heart,
but it is the Lord's purpose that prevails.

Proverbs 19:21 NIV

There are so many more states than provinces. If you blinked you might miss a state or two while driving. So we drove through Massachusetts and New York State. We spent the night in a hotel in Buffalo on the Canadian border where Fred ditched his fatigues (Air Force issue uniform). We laughed about this because we envisioned the maids finding them and assuming an American soldier had deserted to Canada. We drove through Pennsylvania and then crossed into the State of Ohio. I was absolutely dumbfounded that there was no snow on the ground and this was winter. I could not fathom a world without snow in January! I could not believe there were no sub-zero temperatures either. In my tunnel worldview, winter was everywhere in the world. We study geography in school but do not comprehend or grasp the differences until we experience them. We kept driving south speculating on the kind of life that awaited us. We were clueless.

We stopped at a gas station right after crossing into Kentucky I knew we had definitely crossed the imaginary Mason-Dixon Line which separates the north from the south of the United States because I had my first encounter with the southern accent. I am sorry to say that as soon as the service station attendant opened his mouth I laughed hilariously. Now remember this was in the day when self-service had not been instituted yet. I knew this was a 'faux pas' to laugh at people but it was the funniest 'twang' I had ever heard. It was even stronger than what I had heard in the movies or on TV. This was the real deal! We had crossed the north-south bridge with all of its history and heritage. I was remembering the American history course I took while a college student in Canada, and how I had been deeply moved then by the plight of the slaves, and greatly admired Abraham Lincoln for his accomplishments through the secession war which ended slavery. It was no longer just words in a history book but I was feeling the awe of this historical moment.

Excitement was building! We were getting closer to Memphis, our new home! The first thing you see when you go downtown in Memphis Tennessee is a beautiful bridge in the shape of a giant M spanning the Mississippi River. What a beautiful sight especially at night with the lights contouring its shape giving the city a striking skyline, and right next to it you see a giant pyramid, a sports arena. So we arrived in the 'city of good abode' hauling all of our worldly possessions which did not amount to much because we had sold most of them before leaving Massachusetts. We had resigned ourselves with much chagrin to the fact that we would not be returning to Canada. We were going to make the best of this new life in Memphis Tennessee.

What a blessing when we rolled into Fred's parents' driveway and I met his family for the first time! His mother, Lois, was a sweet southern belle with a very thick southern accent. She was such a dear, the most giving person I had ever known. His father and his siblings: two brothers, David and Ricky, and a sister, Ginger, were warm and friendly. We stayed with them for a week while we looked for an apartment. We were in the process of building a bridge to civilian life. What an adjustment! Staying with Fred's family was fun. I experienced true southern hospitality. This is where I was introduced to southern living and southern cuisine like black-eyed peas, barbecued pork, yams with marshmallows, and fried catfish, just to name a few. These foods are delicious and have become my favorites to this day.

I again experienced culture shock where language was concerned! Fred and I had gotten use to the 'Yankee' northern accent along with the slang expressions and acronyms which was like speaking in a code. We did figure out what the people were saying since we were immersed in that culture for over six months, and that is what it takes to learn a foreign language, even another form of English.

When we arrived in Memphis, Fred had no problem communicating since this is where he was born and reared. He just clicked right in, the accent, the southern English language expressions and various dialects posed no problems for him. On the other hand, I struggled to understand the people. I could not grasp or connect with what any of the people were saying to me. I would have them repeat several times, to the point that I was embarrassed by the leery looks I got, so I would finally just agree with them. I am sure they must have thought I was totally deaf or ignorant. What was so funny at the time was that we were all speaking English or some form of English: southern American English, African American English, southern belle English, street talk, and all of it seemed so foreign to me. The laughter that I unleashed over my pronunciation due to the French Canadian or British interference made me just want to crawl under a table or simply remain silent. I really felt like an outsider, an alien from another planet, that I did not belong and I was wondering if I ever would. I had not realized that even though Canada and the US share the same border, share a similar culture and language, seem to be a lot alike on the surface and yet they were so different. What an eye opener! There were times when I would begin to speak French like I did when we were in Massachusetts, and I then would suddenly realize where I was. What a confusing time! I truly have empathy for emigrants. I felt totally isolated and alone. I had no friends. Nothing seemed familiar to me. The excitement of this move was totally gone. I was extremely unhappy and wishing I were back in Canada. I was homesick for anything familiar. I was miserable.

Another factor in my initiation to the southern culture was the heat and the humidity in the summer time. It was a total shock to my system. Fred would have to turn the air conditioner on in the car for it to cool off and then I would jump in, go to where I needed to go, jump out and run into the air conditioned establishment, other wise I would not have survived. I found out that swimming pools are not a luxury but a relief in the south! We have a pool and I have taught our children and grandchildren to swim. By the way, our pool is much warmer than the river we swam in while in Canada. I remember taking Fred to experience swimming in our Iroquois river beside the Trans-Canada. When he jumped into the frigid water, he turned blue and sank. I thought I had killed him. I did not know any better, I assumed all swimming holes were that cold. However, I have learned to endure the summer heat just knowing that I don't have to live through another harsh winter with five months of snow on the ground that has to shoveled and the sub-zero temperatures. I am perfectly happy knowing that as long as I can go skiing once a year, my snow and cold weather satisfaction are quenched.

With the early discharge, Fred was able to return to the University of Memphis in order to finish his business degree on the G.I. bill (General Issue - Military Funding). Thank You Uncle Sam! The Veterans Administration found him employment at the Federal Reserve Bank in

Memphis working on computers all night, the graveyard shift, so that he could attend classes in the mornings. It was a rough and demanding schedule. There were no other choices.

The only work I was able to find when we first arrived was to be a checker in a large grocery store chain 'Giant Foods'. Scanners had not been invented yet so I had to punch in all the prices manually. What an experience! It was challenging work with long hours and heavy lifting. This is where I was introduced to all kinds of southern produce which I had never seen before. There were collard greens, turnip greens, poke salad greens and all kinds of greens. There were sweet potatoes, black eyed peas, and a bunch of other peas. I was a potatoes, carrots, broccoli, cabbage and parsnips person. I knew apples and berries since they grew wild in New Brunswick. I did enjoy meeting people. The business of the job was a big plus because it made the time to go by quicker and kept my mind off being homesick.

Within a year, I was able to obtain a temporary two year Teacher's License from the State of Tennessee allowing me to teach in a private elementary Catholic school. I taught fifth grade the first year and sixth grade the second year. I was elated and I felt human again because I was doing what I was called to do. Teaching was my DNA. Ever since the time I can remember as a child growing up, I would always state emphatically that I was going to be a teacher when I grew up and when I played school – guess who the teacher was? Me of course! My parents would always introduce me as 'the teacher' because they would always agree with my faith confession. Psychologists call it the self-fulfilling prophesy. There is power in our words and that is why it is important to speak positively over our children rather than tear them down. We should always be careful about what we say and how we say it because it could be detrimental to the mental health of anyone including ourselves.

Prov 18:21 *Words kill, words give life; they're either poison or fruit — you choose.*

Building the bridge from the military to civilian life had been quite an adjustment. We were also building one from living in the north to living in the south. Fred was extremely busy going to university and working nights. I was busy teaching again, doing what I was created to do so that was very fulfilling and rewarding. I was finally beginning to feel like I belonged somewhere. We were slowly but surely settling into our new civilian normal lifestyle.

In the midst of our becoming a more southern couple, we would sometimes think out loud and dream about going back to Canada. The thought of returning was always back to where I was born and reared, the real east, because that is all we knew. Even I would wonder and almost worry about how Fred would fit in with it being so very French. I had never been out west so in my mind, I assumed all of Canada was like where I was from. We get tunnel vision about our environment and process the world through that one worldview we know. We assume our experience is the only one. We do not even realize we are that way until we are thrust into another culture. Traveling is good. Everyone needs to see how the other half live as the saying goes. So this is where we were at that time and I should add we were content.

CHAPTER 5

THE RECONCILIATION BRIDGE
FRESH START

Now we look inside,
and what we see is that anyone united
with the Messiah gets a fresh start, is created new.

2 Corinthians 5:17

We only had six months together in Massachusetts to adjust to being together again before moving to Memphis. I have to be honest. Too much change too soon! The newness and excitement were gone. I was homesick and feeling even further away from my family and my homeland, and I began to realize that Canada was not going to happen. The finality of it was settling in my soul. Not only relocating to a new environment difficult and our different working schedules, we were still learning and adjusting to our roles as husband and wife. A whole year apart had caused us to be independent of each other. We had written every day but it was not like living together. It is easy to be nice and loving in letters but living together is another story. Putting those attributes into practice was extremely demanding. We were learning to die to our selfishness. We were learning to put the other's needs first.

Fred was going to university in the mornings, sleeping in the afternoons and working the late night shift. I was teaching school in the day and we had a few hours together in the evenings before he would go to work all night. At first we were satisfied with just each other's company and did not feel a need to have friends. We had tried to be everything to each other and seemed to be succeeding. We were setting each other up for a fall as an idol in one another's life. I guess being apart so much drove us to have that kind of mentality. We just wanted each other and no one else. Between trying to hold on to each other excessively and our weird schedules, we began to grow apart. Our marriage began to break down. We had not built our house on God's way as depicted in the Gospel of Matthew.

Matthew 7:24-27 *"These words I speak to you are not*

incidental additions to your life, homeowner improvements to your standard of living. They are foundational words, words to build a life on. If you work these words into your life, you are like a smart carpenter who built his house on solid rock. Rain poured down, the river flooded, a tornado hit — but nothing moved that house. It was fixed to the rock. "But if you just use my words in Bible studies and don't work them into your life, you are like a stupid carpenter who built his house on the sandy beach. When a storm rolled in and the waves came up, it collapsed like a house of cards."

We were no longer happy with each other and we were not meeting each others needs anymore. We had lost our way and it was as if we were stumbling around in the dark – which we were. We felt like we were in a dead end situation with no where to go. We were struggling financially too. Life was just not fun! No one person can satisfy totally, only God whom we did not know intimately yet. We were lonely and bored because we had no social life. We had no friendships outside of work, I had my co-workers at school and Fred had his co-workers at the bank. That was the sum total of our relationships besides each other. We needed 'couple' friends which we did not have and there was no opportunity to make any because of our schedules. We were not in church or any group or community where we could have built some lasting friendships. There was no accountability in our lives. We were lost souls totally consumed with wanting to be happy and looking for it in all the wrong places. We were selfish, self-centered, and self-consumed with what we wanted individually. At the same time, there was a longing in our souls that could not be quenched. The honeymoon was definitely over! We merely existed. We loved each other but did not know how to live and function together anymore. We needed God to fix us.

I did not know how to pray but I called out to God the only way I knew how which was by reciting the Serenity Prayer by an unknown author that I had found in an Ann Landers column in the newspaper. It goes like this:
God, grant me the Serenity to accept the things I cannot change, Courage to change the things I can, and Wisdom to know the difference.

It gave me comfort. The memorized ritualistic prayers I had learned growing up brought me no peace. I had been in Memphis for about two and a half years when I decided it was time to call it quits. I was tired of being miserable so I flew home to Canada to be with my family. Divorce was the only answer! I was done! I would start all over again. I felt totally humiliated and broken hearted over this failure. I thought I was another statistic of a Canadian girl marrying an American airman that ended in 'splitsville'.

I was welcomed home by my family with a bleeding heart and a shattered dream. As soon as I arrived, my mother told me to keep my mouth shut because I would live to regret it. She knew I was angry at Fred and I just wanted to retaliate because of all the hurt and disappointment I was experiencing. I wanted to blame him for everything but in reality it takes two to tango. The next day, Fred called me and asked forgiveness and wanted me to come home. I set three conditions that he had to agree to before in order for me to return to Memphis. The first one was that we should go to church. I had watched his parents and they were happy with each other, had a prosperous life in every aspect, and had wonderful friends. I came to the conclusion that the one variable that caused all of this was because they went to church regularly, so we needed to do the same. The second one was that he had to find a day job so we could have time together and lead a normal life. The third stipulation was that it was time to start a family because I wanted to be a mother. To my surprise he agreed to all three of them.

Fred's precious grandma, whom we called Nana, wrote me a letter while I was in Canada. She told me she was praying for me and that God loved me. No one had ever told me they were praying for me. Those words so affected me that I wept uncontrollably. It was as though all the pain was being washed away and a deep healing in my soul was taking place. I believe this letter tenderized my heart towards God. I was still quoting the serenity prayer because it was still the only prayer that I knew. God was drawing me to Himself through this prayer. He knows how to reach each one of us when we will call on Him. It is in brokenness that we begin to look up.

I flew back to Memphis about ten days later and we reconciled. It was the most precious homecoming that I had ever experienced! And what ensued was another honeymoon which was absolutely wonderful. It was like we had gotten married all over again. We were given a second chance and we were elated because deep down we really loved each other and had never stopped. We definitely wanted a future together because we had always said that it was our fate. We knew we were meant to spend the rest of our lives together. We did not understand the concept of destiny yet. We did not grasp the idea that God had a plan for our lives to serve Him together. We were building the reconciliation bridge under God's direction.

CHAPTER 6

THE MINISTRY BRIDGE
THE CALL TO PASTOR

"Before I shaped you in the womb,
I knew all about you.
Before you saw the light of day,
I had holy plans for you:

Jeremiah 1:5

W e were determined in our hearts that our marriage was going to work. We were never going to separate again because it was the most miserable and painful time in our lives. Death would have been easier. Our total dependence on each other had to shift to a dependence on God because we had made idols of each other due to our own insecurities. God said in Exodus 20:3 *No other gods, only me.* We had looked to each other to fulfill our every need which brought temporary relief rather than a lasting peace.

So here we are learning to become one in spirit, soul, and body. It does not mean we lose our individual identities but it does mean we both had to submit to God in order to be able to be the husband and wife God wanted us to be. We needed to learn to be selfless rather than selfish, Christ-centered rather than self-centered by serving one another which only comes by dying to our self-will.

Eph 5:21-23 *Out of respect for Christ, be courteously reverent to one another. Wives, understand and support your husbands in ways that show your support for Christ. The husband provides leadership to his wife the way Christ does to his church, not by domineering but by cherishing.*

Because of the lack of trust I had for Fred, I watched him closely and I was thinking at that time that if he reneges on any of the promises he made to me, I would leave. I really did not want to leave. I loved him and I wanted my marriage to work. He changed to a day job, we started attending church with his parents, and I soon found I was with child. I thank God that Fred kept his word. He proved to be a man of integrity and character for which I am grateful to this day. There were times when married life was difficult but we were learning to trust each other again. God was working in us and teaching us to die to ourselves.

We regularly attended the Methodist church on Sundays and I watched Fred and was impressed because he knew how to do church. He knew all the hymns, prayers and creeds that were used in each service. He also knew when to stand and he seemed so holy. I was impressed because I had never seen that side of him before. I was enjoying the peace and security I was feeling. I understand now why I felt that way. When a husband takes the spiritual lead in the home it brings in God's order and He can bless that relationship and everything about it.

We loved going to a restaurant with his family and their friends after service. We were building relationships and it was wonderful. We loved the atmosphere of belonging and the feeling of community we had been hungering for. The people were so very loving and kind and had accepted me, a foreigner. Needless to say, the longing in our souls for acceptance and love were being fulfilled and satisfied. God did not mean for us to do life alone but within His family, the church.

Christopher Lee Bennett was born almost nine months to the day after we had reconciled. His name means 'Christ bearer' which was very appropriate because God used him to lead us to Him. Something happens when you have a child. You realize that you are now responsible for another life rather than just yourselves. We dedicated him to the Lord in the Methodist Church when he was about six months old and promised to rear him in the faith.

Later that year, we received a church directory and Fred's and Chris' names were in it but not mine. I was truly offended and was told when I inquired that I had never officially joined the church. This was a foreign concept to me being reared Catholic because I had never seen people join the church I grew up in, they were born into it. I assumed that because I attended regularly that I was automatically a member. Needless to say I joined since I desperately needed to be a part of that wonderful community that had so embraced me.

We both loved to sing so we joined the choir which was an easy step in our commitment to the church. His mother was the pianist and his father sang and also helped direct the choir. It was another way of building relationships with fellow members. We were flourishing. Our social life was centered on church life and I loved every moment of it. We even began to attend Sunday school and I enjoyed learning about the Bible because I knew nothing since my religious upbringing centered on catechism. I was like a blank slate and God's word was being etched on my brain. I was enjoying learning since I have always been an avid student. Fred was very knowledgeable of the Bible and I could ask him anything concerning the Scriptures and he knew the answers. That really impressed me. He could debate Scripture with people to the point of embarrassing me. He had the gift of gab even back then!

We were being restored to wholeness in our personal lives and in our marriage. Our lifestyles were being transformed because we were learning to incorporate Christ's teachings into every aspect of our lives, and by the community of believers we were building relationships with. This was evidenced by the new godly behaviors and habits we were exhibiting. His nature was becoming ours. We were experiencing victory. His methods are guaranteed to bring lasting results. Our worldview was changing to His Biblical worldview. The Bible calls it mind renewal. We were being molded into the Christian culture daily and we were becoming kingdom minded.

Romans 12:2 *Don't become so well-adjusted to your culture that you fit into it without even thinking. Instead, fix your attention on God. You'll be changed from the inside out. Readily recognize what he wants from you, and quickly respond to it. Unlike the culture around you, always dragging you down to its level of immaturity, God brings the best out of you, develops well-formed maturity in you.*

Life was good again and we were happy. We were so hungry for truth that it made us seekers. We knew about God. We were building a bridge to salvation. God was processing us. We were in the right place at the right time. We human beings all need to come to the realization that we were born into some sort of dysfunctional background because of this fallen sinful world we live in. Only God through Christ Jesus can make us whole and holy. God is in the business of redemption. He remains constant whereas culture constantly changes.

So a year and a half later a new pastor was sent to this church. There were rumors that he was Spirit-Filled although we had no clue as to what that meant. He was different in that when he prayed he would unashamedly kneel down on the platform with hands extended to heaven and talk to God extemporaneously as if he were alone in the room with Him. He never recited memorized prayers nor did he read them out of a book of prayer which intrigued us. He was so joyful and it showed in his attitude and actions. We were drawn to him or so we thought when in actuality it was God in him. We inquired and he told us the reason was that he was 'born again' and in love with His Maker. We wanted to know what that meant and have that same feeling and outlook on life.

One particular Sunday in 1975, I was so moved by the message that I ran down to the chancel rail which is sometimes called the altar in Protestant churches. I prayed the 'sinner's prayer'. In other words I repented and renounced my self-centered and selfish way of life and chose to be a follower of Jesus Christ's teachings. I was encouraged to talk to God regularly, that is prayer, and to read my Bible so that I could get to know Him and His ways. From that moment on I began to change in attitude and actions. Fred had been experiencing the same exact thing. Our faith walk has always been a simultaneous one. We have always liked doing things together and whenever one of us would slack off the other would be there to encourage, not necessarily with words but by our faith in action.

Not long after this experience there was a 'Lay-Witness Mission' in our church where lay people came in for a weekend at the invitation of our pastor, and shared their journey of faith, their story, on how God had touched them and changed them. It was most intriguing! We were curious and a little skeptical, like doubting Thomas in the Bible who would only believe Jesus' crucifixion unless he saw the holes in his hands and feet. One particular lady had shared how God had baptized her with the Holy Spirit and how God healed her leg since she had been in a terrible car accident that had left her almost crippled. He healed and lengthened it and later on she began to participate in beauty pageants in order to be a witness of His healing power. Through her faith we were encouraged and mentored into the fullness of God's Spirit.

After that encounter with God, we had such a desire and a hunger to serve Him and His people in the church. We crossed another bridge. We were totally sold out to becoming followers of the teachings of Christ. We experienced God's power through the infilling of His Holy Spirit in our lives and His character: love, joy, peace, patience, kindness, gentleness, goodness, faithfulness, and self-control. (Gal 5: 22-23) We found ourselves wanting to lead others across this same bridge.

Two years into this walk, I wanted a blue-eyed blond-haired daughter. Lo and behold, God did it! I found a verse in the Bible which I am paraphrasing that said if I delighted in God He would give me the desire of my heart (Psalm 37:4). What jubilation on delivery day! Valerie Denise Bennett was born. My girl! People could not believe it because I had been thanking God for my daughter all these months and there she was. There were no sonograms in those days to detect the gender of the child while in the womb. She was a delight, a very easy and compliant child who always loved praise music. I believe God called her to be a worshiper from the very beginning of her life and that is why He is using her in this ministry along side her husband, Jeremy, a worship leader and recording artist.

God was equipping us for service by enhancing our gifts. Unbeknownst to us, He was preparing us to build a bridge to the ministry, that of being pastors. Fred was appointed the Lay Leader of the Methodist church which is like the position of an associate pastor. We found ourselves very involved in many aspects of the ministry through teaching, serving and loving the people. We enjoyed every minute of it. We had purpose and were fulfilled.

I already knew Fred was called to the ministry when he told me and I rejected the call. I wrestled with this idea of being pastors for a whole year and I just could not see myself in that role. I had not married a minister. I was not called to be a nun married to a priest. What would my family and friends say! I was perfectly happy serving in a lay ministry capacity. Finally my inner turmoil sent me to our Pastor to seek counsel and I told him he must convince Fred not to 'cross the bridge' of ministry. Deep down I was feeling insecure and fearful at losing my position with my husband. I was being selfish. I did not realize that loving God above all else gave us more love for each other. We were learning how to function as spouses according to the word of God.

Colossians 3:18-19 AMP *Wives, be subject to your husbands [subordinate and adapt yourselves to them], as is right and fitting and your proper duty in the Lord. Husbands, love your wives [be affectionate and sympathetic with them] and do not be harsh or bitter or resentful toward them.*

Fred never coerced me into accepting the call. He waited patiently for a whole year which is not his nature. He tends to be highly motivated and focused when he has a goal to accomplish. I know this had to be God! Finally I heard God speak to my heart and He let me know that I was called along side of him. The fear that I had felt left me and was replaced by a perfect peace. I knew that I knew we were both called. That settled it for me.

We told our pastor we were ready to accept the call on our lives. In 1978, he blessed us and sent us out to take on our first charge: Piperton United Methodist Church just outside of Memphis. It was a little country church with about thirty-five elderly people. We crossed and built the ministry bridge with our children. Chris was four years old at the time and Denise was one. We were beginning a new phase of life; that of being pastors of a local church. We were excited! Who would have thought! Fred and Val pastors! God has a sense of humor!

Ephesians 2:10 *God does both the making and saving. He creates each of us by Christ Jesus to join him in the work he does, the good work he has gotten ready for us to do, work we had better be doing.*

CHAPTER 7

THE DENOMINATIONAL BRIDGE
PIPERTON UNITED METHODIST CHURCH

*The goal is for all of them to become one heart and
mind - Just as you, Father, are in me and I in you,
So they might be one heart and mind with us.
Then the world might believe that you, in fact, sent me.*

John 17:21

When Val and I answered the call to ministry in our United Methodist Church, neither one of us had any inkling as to the kinds of relationships we might have with other pastors in our own denomination. No one in either of our families had ever been in ministry so we only knew about the ministry in a very superficial and idealistic way. We dearly loved our pastor who agreed to recommend us for the ministry but once we were gone it seemed to be "out of sight, out of mind." We had to rely totally on the Holy Spirit.

Now don't misunderstand me here. I'm certainly not criticizing him. The Lord used him to introduce us to so many things including salvation; the person of the Holy Spirit; and the opportunity to minister under his supervision. Rev. Everett Roseberry will always have a special place in our hearts! But in the denominational hierarchy the task of guiding and mentoring student pastors was given to District Superintendents.

Piperton United Methodist Church was our first pastoral assignment. As I was going to school at the time, I was considered a "student pastor." This meant my first priority was to finish my University of Memphis Business Degree and then move on to seminary. Piperton United Methodist was an old family church with a classic rural brick building in a soybean field across the highway from a chemical company. When we arrived there were 35 people in regular attendance and none of them were children. Our two kids were the only ones in the church that first few months.

I will never forget the first gathering of our Memphis-McKendree District pastors and wives. We certainly understood that we were rookies but still we had looked forward to this time with expectancy. After all, we would be with other couples like ourselves who shared a common call and life experience. We were shocked by the negative attitudes which were so prevalent in the group. I don't recall meeting anyone who seemed happy or thankful in their calling! No one bothered to encourage us or offered to befriend or mentor us. It was as if all these pastors were our competitors and not our allies.

The topper came when the pastor of one of the largest and most influential churches in our district, which was the nearest to our little church in a bean field, introduced me to some of the prominent lay leaders in his congregation. He introduced me as the man who had come to stop the growth of their great church. I stood their awkwardly waiting for someone to laugh thinking it was some sort of joke. But when everyone turned and walked away I knew I had just experienced my first baptism of fire in the ministry. I had been put on notice that things would not be so different in the church from the ways of the world much to my chagrin.

Over the years I did meet some great men of God who had a heart for a younger generation of ministers, but they were few and far between. One of them was my District Superintendent Paul Douglass who seemed to genuinely take an interest in me and my welfare. The other was the pastor of the largest UMC in West Tennessee, Maxie Dunnam, who always remembered our names when he would see us at annual conference, the yearly gathering of pastors in the denomination. Both of these men exhibited the traits of servant leaders.

Like most new pastors I began to visit the membership and found out who were their children and then began to visit them. I discovered that most of them had left the church for the same reason that we had as teenagers. They felt the church was irrelevant and insincere, if not outright hypocritical. I needed to build a bridge to where they were if I ever hoped to entice them to come to church. After all, the typical worship services at Piperton United Methodist Church were what most of them had left! So in an effort to build a bridge to this missing generation we started a small home group. In those days there was little or no teaching or material on small groups but I knew that John Wesley, the Methodist pioneer, had used home meetings when the church proved inhospitable to his preaching and to his new converts.

In the home group I was able to close the gap between the church and this younger generation. I introduced contemporary music, a relaxed informal setting, and practical Bible based teaching. Vision was cast for a new kind of church which would more effectively impact the culture in which we lived. This strategy successfully grew the church to eighty-five people.

Prov 29:18 *If people can't see what God is doing, they stumble all over themselves; But when they attend to what he reveals, they are most blessed.*

Word of our small renewal movement began to be "noised abroad" and this opened the door for more growth. As these new people visited our church some of them were willing to open their homes and invite friends and family of like mind and spirit for small group meetings. Sometime during our third year we grew to about a hundred and fifty people.

In our fourth year at Piperton UMC a visitor came to a small group meeting in our home. She informed us that there was another group meeting down the street and she was on her way to that meeting. It was decided that our group would go and visit this new group which was not attached to any church. It would be another act of "bridge building."

When we arrived we were a bit shocked to discover that over forty people were meeting together in this home. They very graciously opened the door of their house and their hearts to us. Carolyn Franklin was the teacher/leader of this group which was made up of Pentecostal people. I remember moving around the large room, really a garage which had been remodeled into a den, and meeting so many interesting people. With several of them the Lord gave me a word of knowledge or encouragement. The room was electric with anticipation as we waited upon the Lord to see what He might do.

I recall that Shirley, a newcomer to our church, was a bit apprehensive about going to a meeting full of Pentecostals. She was from a Baptist background and had been warned about these strange people who delved into the things of the Holy Ghost. As we walked up to the door I tried to comfort her and put her at ease. I said, "Shirley, don't worry about anything. Just stay with us and do what we do." Wouldn't you know that during the meeting a lady would walk across the room toward me and begin to prophesy? I have no idea to this day what she said, but as soon as she opened her mouth I went down. Not in the typical fashion of falling backward, overcome by the Spirit. No! I fell forward landing on a large plastic cube which broke my fall and kept me from breaking my face! As I lay there, unable, unwilling to move, I couldn't help but wonder what our little Baptist girl must be thinking now!

We merged the two groups and within a year practically all of them had joined Piperton UMC. Our fifth and last year saw the church grow to over three hundred and fifty people. Of the hundred who joined that year only two were Methodists. We began to realize that the sign out front was a misnomer because these people were not joining the Methodist Church; they were joining what was a new paradigm church for that day. We had become one of the most denominationally diverse churches in the Memphis area. We had crossed another bridge. It was also in this year that my District Superintendent resigned and guess who they named to replace him? The pastor who had introduced me as the man who had come to stop their church's growth! A man who had no use for me or our church! The handwriting was on the wall and I knew that my days were numbered.

Before I leave this period behind I need to mention the role of media in helping us to bridge the gap from an obscure rural congregation to a new church plant. One of our new members who happened to be a Methodist was married to a man in the broadcast media. He connected me with Lou Harris, the producer of a Sunday morning TV program called "What Is Your Faith?" At first I was an occasional substitute whenever one of the regular panel members was absent. After a few months I became a regular on the program along with six to eight other panelists from denominations as diverse and divergent as Roman Catholic, Greek Orthodox, Methodist, Southern Baptist, Missionary Baptist, Church of Christ, Assembly of God and even Jewish. Viewers wrote to Channel 3, the CBS affiliate in Memphis, and asked questions. A moderator would then present the questions to the panel for discussion. Sometime after the first year or so I became the moderator. This exposure gave us both credibility and invaluable experience with the broadcast media, although it is hard to measure how much it helped our church directly. It certainly has helped us in our ministry over the years and I will be forever grateful to my good friend and television mentor Lou Harris.

We served the Methodist Church for five years from 1978 to 1983. During that time I finished my degree in Business Administration at the University of Memphis and my Master of Divinity at Memphis Theological Seminary, and Val received her Bachelor of Education from the University of Memphis so she could resume her teaching career. I would never recommend any couple going to school at the same time with only one car and two small children. What an experience! God's grace is sufficient and where we are weak He makes us strong. Also during that period we entered our first building program. We added a fellowship hall for special activities and wedding receptions just before the Lord called us out of the Methodist church.

So needless to say that after five years of university and seminary, and serving as a student pastor, we were more than ready for a vacation. We desperately needed the time to withdraw and see things from a different perspective. Some friends kindly invited us to stay in a family home in Florida from which we could commute to both the beach and Disney World. It was a great time for our family as we left the glass bowl of being pastors and just paid attention to one another and our children.

After about a week we began to drive up the eastern seaboard to Virginia Beach, Virginia. When Sunday morning came around Val wanted to visit a church she had been watching on TV. This is a wonderful example of how important Christian media is. Had we not seen this service on television, we would not have gone to Virginia Beach to receive the vision for Christ the Rock Church. So we loaded up the kids and went to Rock Church, a large charismatic church. When we walked in the door of this church in a city we had never been to before, we met someone we knew. This was another divine connection.

Ted Panteleo, now deceased, was a deacon in this great church of several thousand. In those days a Charismatic or Pentecostal church of this size was unusual. Ted graciously found Val and the children seats and took me back to meet the pastors, John, now deceased, and Anne Gimenez. After a brief introduction they invited me to come out onto the platform with them. I wondered what kind of people these were who so freely allowed a stranger to join them on the platform of their church on national television.

What I stepped into that morning was beyond description. Val and the kids watched with unbelief at me standing on the platform. Although we were charismatic, we were still in a Methodist church, so we operated with a certain amount of restraint. But on that platform there was so much freedom in the Holy Spirit that I was awestruck. The music, the choir, the gifts of the spirit and a congregation, like I had never seen before, seemed to swallow me. As I gazed out on that great multitude I was amazed to see people of every ethnicity. People that I had been told could not worship together successfully were worshipping together in the unity of the spirit. In

65

seats of honor on the front row were people who had been brought in off the mean streets that very morning. They had been offered breakfast, a shower and a change of clothes and treated as honored guests.

And then Anne Gimenez began to prophesy. I don't remember the exact words and she was speaking generally to the congregation but Val and I felt she was speaking to us. It was as though the Lord had broken through our doubts and confusion and given us specific instructions. We were to go back to Memphis and pioneer a church which would be a "bridge" to people of all socio-economic levels and ethnicities. What we saw in Virginia Beach could also be found in other cities like St. Louis, Dallas, Atlanta, and across the country. But could it happen in Memphis, a city tormented by racial animosity? The city where Martin Luther King had been assassinated?

Before we left Virginia Beach that day, our friend Ted Panteleo offered me a job with Pat Robertson's ministry. We were big fans of the 700 Club and were thrilled and honored to be offered a position with this international ministry. The dilemma, founding a diverse church or going to work for Pat Robertson! For two days as we traveled back to Memphis, we wrestled with the choice of moving to Virginia Beach and working in the political arm of Pat Robertson's ministry or going back to Memphis to plant a new church. I have always loved politics. Val said that if I hadn't become a preacher I would have been a great politician. By the time we reached Memphis we knew what we were to do.

Both choices were good but we had to choose what God wanted versus what we would have liked. We had to really examine our hearts. We had to trust God. In retrospect, that ministry did not survive and I would have been without a job / ministry. Before going on vacation, Val had signed a teaching contract with one of the school systems in Memphis. God definitely wanted us to stay in Memphis because He wanted to use us in His overall plan to bring about racial reconciliation to the city.

Proverbs 16:9 NKJV *A man's heart plans his way, But the Lord directs his steps.*

We believe God showed us a great church through the television media and we were led by the Holy Spirit to go to Virginia Beach so that we would see first hand what God wanted to do for the our next phase of ministry. This was truly a divine appointment. We saw a church filled with all kinds of people worshiping together. God was calling us to pioneer this type of church in Memphis Tennessee! He was calling us to raise up a church dedicated to racial reconciliation! We were excited about this new venture. We had "prophetic purpose" again and this is what we came home to tell our folks we felt God was telling us to do. We were going to have to cross another bridge, the one of racial reconciliation.

Habakkuk 2: 3
This vision-message is a witness
pointing to what's coming.
It aches for the coming — it can hardly wait!
And it doesn't lie.
If it seems slow in coming, wait.
It's on its way. It will come right on time.

CHAPTER 8

THE RACIAL RECONCILIATION BRIDGE
CHRIST THE ROCK CHURCH

*In Christ's family there can be no division
into Jew and non-Jew,
slave and free, male and female.
Among us you are all equal,
that is, we are all in a common relationship with Christ.*

Galatians 3:28

As Val and I drove back to Memphis talking about what we had seen and heard, I began to remember the church I had grown up in. It was an all white congregation of course, as all churches in Memphis were totally segregated in the 50's and 60's. Whenever an African American person or family would dare to walk into one of our services, an uproar would ensue. Usually several of the older white men would jump up and walk out while making racist comments. Even as a teenager I knew that something was wrong with this attitude of apartheid in the church of Jesus Christ. While in high school, Val had read the book 'Black Like Me' by John Howard Griffin which depicted the racial injustices in the south. God was preparing our hearts back then to be open to diversity. Our past experiences are never for naught because they always propel us into our future destinies.

We held our first meeting as a nondenominational, spirit filled church in the old VFW (veterans) club in Collierville in July of 1983. It was an interesting place to hold services. There were liquor and beer signs on the wall and the coke machine was filled with Budweiser beers. I preached on a small stage in front of a large bingo board. I used to joke that people in our church didn't say Amen but "bingo" when they agreed! The first Sunday we filled the place and it became apparent that we would have to find a larger meeting place for Sunday morning services.

The old Germantown community center near the High School fit the bill for our growing church. It could easily accommodate two hundred and gave us room to grow while we looked for property. This venue and the VFW only cost us twenty-five dollars per service. The low overhead enabled us to save our money for a future location which we would soon need. At the end of our first year we were running a hundred and fifty on Sunday mornings and had purchased five acres on Houston Levee Road between the suburban towns of Germantown and Collierville. This seemed like a good location as it was accessible to all our members. We paid off the loan in six months and began construction of an all purpose facility which would accommodate five hundred people.

A local bank in Collierville was willing to loan us the money needed for construction because of our attendance, giving levels, and ownership of 5 valuable acres. Our congregation also included some long time residents of Collierville that the bank wanted to please. Even though we were a new congregation with a limited track record the bank viewed our loan application for half a million dollars favorably.

We moved into our new facility in January of 1985. Even though it snowed every weekend that January, which is a real fluke of weather in Memphis, we quickly jumped to two hundred and fifty people. Other than newspaper advertising our main media expenditure was for radio time. Val and I taught a 15 minute program five days a week on a local station which covered the area we were drawing people from. It was called 'A Drink from the Rock'. In those days it was quite novel for a husband and wife to broadcast a religious program. The husband and wife team was a bridge we crossed. We were on the air for six years but for years afterward people would recognize our voices when they heard us talking in public. We were forced off the radio when our station was bought out by an evangelical group which objected to Val, a woman teaching, and our charismatic expressions.

But even this worked for our good because it encouraged us to launch our first television program which ran for five years. We taped our Sunday morning show at a secular station down town Memphis where the camera men and women mocked us. It was like street preaching. Close to the end of our time with them, their hearts had softened because they would ask us to pray for them when they were going through situations in their lives. The seeds we had planted on the air waves had also dropped into their souls. God has used us in the media almost from the beginning of our ministry. Radio first, then television be it a secular station, the local TBN (Christian Network), and the Miracle Channel (only twenty-four hour Christian network in Canada). We have been blessed to be used in that capacity.

In the 70's it was the Charismatic churches that broke out of the box on the issue of race. Christ The Rock Church was no exception although participation by African Americans was very slow to catch on. We built a bridge to them by attending African American pastors' conferences and meetings in the Memphis area in order to show our openness to them. Many times we would be the only whites in the gathering. During the first few years we managed to attract a few African-Americans from out of town who had been in mixed churches in other cities. Local Memphians were slow to catch on to this trend and I'm sure that it retarded our growth.

In 1994, there was a Racial Reconciliation meeting held in Memphis where the leaders from the white and black Pentecostal denominations came together to repent of the sin of racial prejudice and agreed to be reconciled. It was an unprecedented holy convocation. After all, this is the city that had assassinated Dr. Martin Luther King in

1968. It was billed as the Miracle at Memphis. Both sides committed to worship, pray, take communion and be in mission together. This story is recorded in the February 2004 issue of Charisma, a Christian publication. Now forty years later on November of 2008, Barack Obama was elected as our first African-American president. This too is a miracle! Dr. King's dream is gradually coming true. Racial tensions are loosening. He had a key Scripture he often quoted:

Amos 5:24 NKJV *But let justice run down like water, And righteousness like a mighty stream.*

We had grown steadily with a few African-Americans and it was time for more needed space so at the end of our tenth year at the Houston Levee location, we purchased twenty acres on Winchester Road in Memphis which is about two miles away. We made a business decision to postpone the TV ministry because we went into a new building program at our present location. We sold our church to another ministry that allowed us to use it for a year while phase one was being constructed. The building was not completed in time so we had to go to temporary facilities in another location in Memphis. We felt like nomads for seven months. It turned out to be a good thing because we were exposed to another part of town and grew.

November of 1996, we moved into phase one of our new facility on Winchester. What excitement! We did not have to worship in a gym anymore. Every move into a new facility is always a unique challenge for the church. However, we adjusted pretty well. Not much drama! We steadily grew so we added a gym which later was converted to a school to house our Academy.

At this location our vision of diversity was finally beginning to really happen because more and more local African-Americans began trickling in. I even changed my preaching style somewhat to appeal to a more diverse congregation and the worship had some elements of African-American music. Much to my dismay, some of our white folk started leaving. Val and I were bothered by this turn of events because we thought everyone had bought into the vision but apparently not. We came to the conclusion that God was simply balancing us to be more equally diverse.

Ps 2:8 NKJV *Ask of Me, and I will give You The nations for Your inheritance, And the ends of the earth for Your possession.*

Regardless, it was awesome seeing racial reconciliation manifest before our eyes. The people would fellowship together in service and in other venues such as home groups. I am sure some whites had never been in a black homes and vice-versa. People were coming from all over the Metro area to see what was happening at Christ the Rock Church. People could hardly believe what they saw. It was wonderful! Everyone left their biases at the door and we just loved each other and ministered to each other. There were no color lines. It was heaven on earth!

The local CBS affiliate, Channel 3, televised our worship service and interviewed me. Our church was chosen as one of the eleven most influential churches in the city. Why eleven? Aren't most statistics based on ten? We realized that of the eleven churches chosen, five were white and five black and we were the only diverse one. They compared us to a church one would see in Los Angeles, Dallas or Atlanta – but Memphis? We had built a bridge of racial reconciliation. After all, we are all God's children and we were coming together in the unity of the Holy Spirit. The

Scripture we believed in our heart became very real to us because we were seeing it come to life before our very eyes. We never stopped proclaiming it.

Galatians 3:28 *In Christ's family there can be no division into Jew and non-Jew, slave and free, male and female. Among us you are all equal. That is, we are all in a common relationship with Jesus Christ.*

CHAPTER 9

SINGLE TO MARRIED LIFE BRIDGE
OUR CHIDREN'S NUPTIALS

All your children will have God for their teacher —
what a mentor for your children!

Isaiah 54:13

F red and I went to Canada for a Camp Meeting at the Lethbridge Victory Church in 1994 at the invitation of our dear friends, Jerry and Teresa Wolcson. This was to be a divine connection because we met many wonderful people and especially Mervyn and Muriel Mediwake who became our dearest friends. After that meeting, we sent Chris up to a youth conference because he was working in our Academy and serving as an Intern in the Student ministry at Christ the Rock at that time. We wanted to expose him to a Canadian ministry because we felt it was part of his heritage since I am Canadian. He ended up staying at the Mediwake house that weekend.

Needless to say, this is where the connection was made between he and Becky, their daughter, but nothing happened immediately because he was engaged to another girl from Bible school whom I knew was not 'the one' God had for him. Mothers know those things because God gives us strong discernment in order to rear and nurture children. So I said nothing and prayed for God's perfect will in the girl and Chris' life. However at Chris' encouragement, Becky ended up going to the same Bible school Chris had attended. She had a heart for children after having just returned from spending a year in Mexico at an orphanage. Our daughter Denise also decided to go to the same Bible school Chris had attended which surprised us because she was truly an academic student with aspirations to become a school teacher like her mother. Still nothing between Chris and Becky!

We were planning Chris' wedding which was to take place in less than three months when all of a sudden he informs me it was all wrong and that he did not love the girl. He called it off and promised to make monetary restitution to the family which was the honorable thing to do which he did. Thank God for His intervention! To my dismay the very next day I asked him how he was doing and expected him to tell me he was miserable. Instead he said he was totally relieved and that now he could start thinking about Becky. I had no idea who she was. I said, "Who is Becky?" I was planning a visit to see Denise and attend a Women's Conference the Bible school was hosting. Chris decided to come with me to see his sister and visit some of his friends. I happened to run into Muriel, Becky's mother, who was visiting her daughter and there to attend the conference. I told her Chris had cancelled his wedding and that he had come down with me to see his sister. I had not noticed Becky sitting next to her mother. She later informed me that when she heard the news she was suddenly overwhelmed and ran to the nearest ladies room to gain composure. She had told her dad the previous year that she was going to marry Chris. We had no idea! I am telling you all of this so that you can see how God works. He truly does order our steps when we seek to follow Him with a whole heart. It is also very important to pray for our children, that they live God's plan for their life. Marriage after salvation is the next most important decision they will ever make.

We decided to meet for dinner the following night. We noticed Chris and Becky talked and had eyes only for each other. Their hearts were being knit together at that very moment but nothing happened immediately. Later that fall I had a ladies conference with Hazel Hill as the speaker. She quizzed Chris and he told her about Becky Mediwake so she prayed for this relationship to flourish. We went on a ski trip that winter and were invited to the Mediwakes afterwards so Chris and Becky could get together. At first it looked like nothing was happening.

The night before we left, something clicked because what ensued was a year long courtship via the snail mail and telephone. This eventually led to a sweet legal ceremony in our living room before the official one in Lethbridge in the dead of winter. Like father, like son, something about those Canadian girls! It was as though this marriage had been pre-arranged which it was by God. They are a perfect match for the call God had on their lives. God truly blessed Chris with Becky, the wife of his dreams, and one who complements him in ministry. Another bridge was built between the US and Canada!

Proverbs 18:2 *Find a good spouse, you find a good life — and even more: the favor of God!*

During their courtship, Chris joined an itinerant ministry with some fellow students from the Bible school he attended. They traveled all over the US. Their venues were in church services, youth events, and school assemblies. They would conduct workshops and perform skits dealing with family issues and Chris would preach a word that went along with the drama. It was very effective and brought a lot of healing and repentance to families. Within six months of his commitment to this ministry is when he and Becky married and once the tour was completed, they moved to Minneapolis, much to our chagrin, to help plant a church. We thought they would be back in Memphis working with us by serving as associate pastors. God had other plans for them. They ended up remaining in that city for four years.

We questioned God. We did not understand why Chris and Becky had to move away, to leave us. It was heart wrenching because we did not know if they would ever be back. Chris needed to learn and experience some things for himself. He did not need to live in his father's shadow.

God was preparing both he and Becky, equipping and training them up to take over the ministry of Christ the Rock Church one day. They needed to find their own identity in Christ and be established as ministers in their own right, and not just be known as Fred and Val's son and daughter-in-law. They had to learn to totally trust God for themselves and not lean on parents. What's more they needed to hear the call from God for themselves, if they were indeed called to receive this mantle. We had to be out of the way for that to happen, otherwise, as parents, we would have hindered what God wanted to do in them and through them, and also in us. So by faith we released them to the destiny God had for them. We felt like Abraham who had finally gotten the desire of his heart, a son, Isaac, and then God asked him to offer him up as a sacrifice on His altar. That is what we had to do, to totally entrust him to the Lord. We prayed for their prosperity and success. It was so difficult letting go. I was learning to practice what I preach! Let go and let God! Easier said than done! After all, while he was growing up I would tell him that he was dedicated to God because he was the first male child to open my womb. So what was he doing? Serving God! What more could a parent want in a child!

God assured us they would come back one day in His timing. We had no idea when! There were times when we had to fight doubt and unbelief. We missed them terribly. They lived 1700 miles away from us and they were happy serving God in Minneapolis. Why would anybody want to move or make changes when things are going so well! We still believed in our heart that they would one day take over the ministry of Christ the Rock Church. God in His mercy gave us two scriptures to stand on and we quoted them constantly.

Isaiah 60:4 *Look up! Look around! Watch as they gather, watch as they approach you: Your sons coming from great distances, your daughters carried by their nannies.*

Jeremiah 31:16-17 NIV *This is what the Lord says: "Restrain your voice from weeping and your eyes from tears, for your work will be rewarded," declares the Lord. "They will return from the land of the enemy. So there is hope for your future," declares the Lord. "Your children will return to their own land.*

Becky and Chris came home for a visit the summer before they moved back, and I remember beginning to see a longing in their hearts to be back in Memphis. I think at the time they were fighting those feelings. They voiced absolutely nothing but I began to sense change was in the air. God was working behind the scenes, orchestrating His plan.

After having been in Minneapolis almost four years, two events caused them to come to the conclusion that it was time for them to return to Memphis. The first one was the eminent birth of our very first grandbaby, their first child, and extenuating circumstances in the ministry.

Romans 8:28 NIV *And we know that in all things God works for the good of those who love him, who have been called according to his purpose.*

They felt their ministry in that great city was finished and that it was time to come and be a vital part of the ministry at Christ the Rock Church. We were absolutely elated and praised God for answering our prayers. So, Maia was born in November and one month later, in December, God brought them home. When God moves, He moves fast! He is Sovereign and He sets the times and boundaries. We have to remember that when we pray, God may say 'yes', 'no', or 'later', but He does answer.

Acts 17:26 NIV *he determined the times set for them and the exact places where they should live.*

Preparation for the transition was going to begin with Chris coming home. The generational bridge was going to have to be built and we did not realize the cost and the length of time involved. Seven years to be exact! Seven in the Bible means completion or perfection. Chris began working in all areas of the ministry, one at a time, so that he would know and understand the workings of every aspect of the ministry. He brought to the table a new and fresh approach which was desperately needed if we were going to reach this new generation. We could not keep doing things the same old way and expect different results. We were challenged to become relevant to the culture without becoming spiritually irrelevant. We read and studied ministries in order to see what they were doing to reach this post modern generation since they were no longer responding to the way we had been doing things. Apparently, we needed to change not compromise our faith in order to reach them. God's word never changes because it is foundational, but His ways and methods do in order to reach more people.

Because of this new paradigm, we began to see insecurities over position and turf occur amongst some of the pastoral staff who had been with us for a long time. They were not ready for change. They were perfectly content the way things were. The status quo! They were intimidated by Chris' gift and wisdom in ministry matters and his new and fresh approach to the way things ought to be done. In other words, he wanted to kill some sacred cows that needed to die because they had become dead works. God was developing him and growing him up fast. We needed him here.

In 2001, we began to make preparations for the construction of a 3000 seat worship center. This was phase three of the master plan. We used a Stewardship Campaign to help raise the needed funds in order to accomplish this part of the vision God had put in our hearts. This was the last piece of the puzzle that needed to be finished. It would be building number six for us. Construction began in the fall of 2001 and it took a little over a year to complete the structure. We occupied the building fall of 2002. Grandson number 2, Levi, the calm one, was born in the same month. Claire, number three, our drama queen, arrived three years later.

Now I must tell you the 'Denise and Jeremy saga'. She traveled all over North America for a year with the same itinerant evangelistic acting team her brother had. She was the lead actress who performed in the skits depicting family issues. She was excellent. She used to say as a little girl that she would one day be an actress. She may have thought Hollywood but God had other plans. Not long after her arrived home, she attended a gig where she met Jeremy Horn, a songwriter / musician, performing a gig at a local church. They became the best of friends and would hang out together along with other people at the 'Ugly Mug', a church sponsored coffee shop. As a mom, I knew from the very beginning that they were meant to be together, but she could not see it. She even hosted his 21st birthday party at our house and all the guests came in costume representing some famous singer. It was hilarious, but they were always 'just friends'.

They went on several missions trips together. They led praise and worship regularly in chapel services for our Bible school. It seemed like God kept putting them together! They even sang at weddings together. Always as best friends! But if he went on away without telling her, she would be extremely agitated. I would remind her that they were not a couple. I got so tired of the yo-yo feelings she had for him. One day she would say he is it and the next, no way! As a mom, I got to ride the roller coaster of emotions with her. Some of you moms can relate to this! I prayed constantly that she would know her heart where this boy was concerned. I knew he loved my daughter and I felt sorry for him because of the bumpy road he was walking on waiting for her to commit to him.

Not long after that, he went on a missions trip without her. I asked God to let her long for him while he was gone – that way she would be able to see her heart. I noticed that he called her each day and I could see she was elated and began acting like someone in love. I dared not get my hopes up! Then he came home and nothing. What is up with that? Finally, Jeremy got enough nerve and confronted her. He told her he was tired of being 'on pause' and that she needed to make up her mind once and for all as to whether or not he fit into her life. It shook her to the very core of her being, and cause her to come to the realization that she did love him and wanted to spend the rest of her life with him. She also realized it was a choice she had to make. Many young people expect a flashing light from God to tell them that a particular person is 'the one'. Others live in fear of making the wrong choice. It still takes faith and being ready to take that step leading to marriage. They had known each other well over four years when they finally hooked up.

Song 2:7 *don't excite love, don't stir it up, until the time is ripe — and you're ready.*

86

Seven months later, they married in the new worship center with over a thousand in attendance. It was the most celebrated wedding I have ever attended. So much joy expressed with laughter and tears! Erica Youngblood sang 'At Last' by Etta James as the bridesmaids made their way down the aisle, and at the end, for the dismissal song, it was 'She Loves You' by the Beatles. What goes around comes around! Fred and I were Beatle fans in the 60's. Jeremy and Denise are a perfect match for the ministry God has called them to. They are artsy, spiritual and never meet strangers. That is why God called them to do praise and worship, lead the student ministry, and the college and career age young people. They have blessed us with two precious spiky blond haired boys, Judah and Liam.

It is important to see how God moves in our children and that is why I am sharing their stories with you hoping you will gain insight concerning your children. I cannot emphasize enough that as parents we must pray for our children's spouses even when they are very young because the right one will either help or hinder them fulfill the call of God on their lives. God did say in Genesis that it was not good for man to be alone so He gave Eve to Adam. In the New Testament Jesus sent His disciples out two by two to do the work of the ministry. God does want spouses working together in the ministry He calls them to.

Ecclesiastes 4:8, 12 NIV *Two are better than one, because they have a good return for their work; if one falls down, his friend can help him up. Though one may be overpowered, two can defend themselves.*

We as parents must train our children in the way that they should go, not the way we went or wished we had gone. Some parents try to relive their lives through their kids and others try to manipulate them to do what they want. Proverbs 22:6 *Point your kids in the right direction — when they're old they won't be lost.*

But we must also live exemplary lives before them. Too many grow up and leave the church because of the hypocrisy they see in us as parents. They don't expect us to be perfect but to be authentic. After all we have the Perfect One abiding inside of us, guiding us. Even when we act in the flesh, we should be quick to apologize to them and not frustrate them.

Ephisians 6:4 *And now a word to you parents. Don't keep on scolding and nagging your children, making them angry and resentful. Rather, bring them up with the loving discipline the Lord himself approves, with suggestions and godly advice.*

It truly is a noble calling and a privilege to have and to rear children which results in grandchildren, the pay-off! Hallelujah! We have five and what a blessing they are! God knew what He was doing when He gave grandchildren at our age. They free our minds from the drama of life by causing us to remain focused on them while caring for them.

Proverbs 17:6 *An old man's grandchildren are his crowning glory. A child's glory is his father.*
Proverbs 13:22 *A good life gets passed on to the grandchildren;*

Chris and Denise grew up as PK's (Preacher's Kids) which means in the eyes of the congregation they should be perfect. Wrong! They are children who have the same issues every other kid has. We wanted them to have a normal life, and we tried to protect them from church politics by never discussing issues or talking about people in front of them. We did not want them to become jaded or skeptical about Christianity. We simply wanted them to love God and His people and live an authentic life. We tried to live and put into practice what God said in the Bible. We reared our children on a Biblical worldview.

Deuteuronomy 6:5-9 *Love God, your God, with your whole heart: love him with all that's in you, love him with all you've got! Write these commandments that I've given you today on your hearts. Get them inside of you and then get them inside your children. Talk about them wherever you are, sitting at home or walking in the street; talk about them from the time you get up in the morning to when you fall into bed at night. Tie them on your hands and foreheads as a reminder; inscribe them on the doorposts of your homes and on your city gates.*

God is the one who blesses us with children and He calls us to be parents, not their best friends, and expects us to fulfill our role as leaders, providers and nurturers of these entrusted gifts. He knows exactly what we will be going through on this journey with them and has promised to never leave or forsake us but to help us. We should never look at our children as burdens even if at times they seem to be. We should trust Him with them and believe and declare that they will turn out all right!

God gave me this verse for Chris. Luke 2:23 *"Every male who opens the womb shall be a holy offering to God,"* I often reminded him that God called him to do great things for Him. He would smile at me.

And for Denise. Psalms 37:4 NIV *Delight yourself in the Lord and he will give you the desires of your heart.* I would tell her often that she was God's desire, and how very special to me and to God she was.

I exhort you parents to ask God to give you a Scripture you can stand on where your children are concerned and remind them often. It does not matter how old they are. God's word works and never returns without accomplishing what it says it will because it is living and powerful.

God was preparing our children to take over the ministry one day. He was telling us to prepare a bridge to the next generation. All through the Bible we see how God used families to bring about His purposes in the earth. We also see that if He can get His ways to three generations, He can get it to thousands. He used Abraham, Isaac, and Jacob who became Israel, a nation. What a promise! We do not have to accept what the world says about our children - that they must sow their wild oats before they finally serve Him. We refused that lie. We taught our children to be givers. Even when they were little, we taught them to tithe their allowance which was but one dollar at the time. They boast in the Lord today that they have always tithed, and because of this practice, they see the correlation that God has always provided for them in every area of their lives. It is good to serve God.

Matthew 6:30-33 *"If God gives such attention to the appearance of wildflowers — most of which are never even seen — don't you think he'll attend to you, take pride in you, do his best for you? What I'm trying to do here is to get you to relax, to not be so preoccupied with getting, so you can respond to God's giving. People who don't know God and the way he works fuss over these things, but you know both God and how he works. Steep your life in God-reality, God-initiative, God-provisions. Don't worry about missing out. You'll find all your everyday human concerns will be met. "Give your entire attention to what God is doing right now, and don't get worked up about what may or may not happen tomorrow. God will help you deal with whatever hard things come up when the time comes.*

CHAPTER 10

THE GENERATIONAL BRIDGE
OUR POSTERITY

"As for me," God says, "this is my covenant with them: My Spirit that I've placed upon you and the words that I've given you to speak, they're not going to leave your mouths nor the mouths of your children nor the mouths of your grandchildren.

Isaiah 59:21

Octavia 2002! The new three thousand seat Worship Center is completed. What joy! What excitement! The fulfillment of a vision God had given us many years ago! A place big enough to house everybody at once in one worship service! A place where there would be synergy because of the intensity and numbers worshipping our Lord Jesus Christ in unity of the Spirit and truth. It would be a testimony to Memphis, a church with all kinds of people depicting the Kingdom of God! A picture of diversity we saw years ago in Virginia Beach. Praise God!

Over the last 30 years we have been involved in building several buildings beginning with a modest fellowship hall for the Methodist church where we served for five years. When Christ the Rock was founded in Collierville, we led the congregation in the construction of two buildings. Then when Christ the Rock moved to its current location the Lord instructed us to contract with the Messner Construction Company for a master plan that was built in three phases. Messner was the last contractor interviewed and even though we had no intention of using an out of town company, the Lord spoke so clearly to the building committee that we had to obey. We also used a Capital Funds Crusade to raise the money for the project. Looking back now, we should have faithed it out. Charismatic churches are not very good at using plans like this. We actually lost a few people for engaging in this program.

The project was so large that we had to build it in phases as the church grew. Graciously, the Lord caused the church to grow in numbers and finances so that the whole project took about eight years. We know the cost involved spiritually, emotionally, and physically in pioneering a new work and growing an existing one. It took the gift of faith to obey and trust Him completely. After all, faith is what moves God to action because it pleases Him. We have learned over the years what to do and what not to do, sometimes the hard way! Growth is always a process over time.

2 Peter 3:18 says, *Grow in grace and understanding of our Master and Savior, Jesus Christ.* Growth is a process which takes time. Grace is God's divine enablement which comes by doing and understanding God's word which causes a mind change. It was a tremendous challenge for a church with pastors like ourselves from such humble beginnings to keep growing because we did not come from a heritage of ministry. Memphis had never seen a charismatic church grow like this and many in the charismatic community were not convinced that such growth was desirable, much less the will of God.

The body of Christ needed a shift in mindset because God's thoughts and ways are always higher than ours. We needed to line up with Him.

Isaiah 55:8-9 NIV *"For my thoughts are not your thoughts neither are your ways my ways," declares the Lord. "As the heavens are higher than the earth, so are my ways higher than your ways and my thoughts than your thoughts.* His way of thinking, influences our actions. The Bible also tells us we have the mind of Christ. So how do we learn to make this shift in our thinking? We have always endeavored to walk in the light by obeying His voice and being led by His Spirit in order to make the necessary shifts. However, learning can be acquired three ways: through experience where success and failure occur, formal education by submitting to school, and then direct impartation. The first two are expensive, time consuming, lots of hard work and dying to self, whereas impartation is instantaneous and easiest to receive because it just happens. No work required! Guess which one people prefer? Some people have said that we tend to always know how to reinvent ourselves. This statement simply means that we have made the necessary adjustments in order to follow God. We thank Him because He has always protected us from harm, and most of all from ourselves.

So here we are in this new Worship Center. We thought this was it! We had arrived! We would continue growing and truly become a loud voice influencing the city of Memphis. We believed God was going to raise up a mighty army to do this. But a funny thing happened on the way to our glorious future! We met some opposition and that is what happens whenever one goes against the status quo.

We remember standing on the platform at that first service in the new beautiful worship center and thinking that we should be more excited than this. We had dreamed of this day. There was a spirit of heaviness instead of a spirit of joy over the accomplishment. In fact we were exhausted from the warfare we had encountered right before the grand opening. There was underlying dissension in the leadership. There were rumors of some of them going out to plant a new work which caused some of the members to be polarized bringing confusion in the ranks. There was competition among the various ministries for the same people. This was not the time for this kind of talk which would only cause a church split we could ill afford.

1 Cor 3:2-4 NIV *You are still worldly. For since there is jealousy and quarreling among you, are you not worldly? Are*

you not acting like mere men? 4 For when one says, "I follow Paul," and another, "I follow Apollos," are you not mere men?

We needed to be in unity above all else. The congregants needed to see unity amongst the leaders otherwise there would be no blessings from God. He indwells a body in one accord.

Ps 133:1-3 *How wonderful, how beautiful, when brothers and sisters get along! It's like costly anointing oil flowing down head and beard, Flowing down Aaron's beard, flowing down the collar of his priestly robes. It's like the dew on Mount Hermon flowing down the slopes of Zion. Yes, that's where God commands the blessing, ordains eternal life.*

It felt like this building was not for us, and that our days were numbered. Years later, our dear friend, Judith Carson, told me that God had told her we had built this building for our son Chris. He would be mightily used by God and he would fill it up. We are living to see that day.

Our vision is and has always been about being a church of all kinds of people, a picture of Heaven on earth, by being reconciled to God first and then to one another. As ministers of the Gospel, our God-given task is to equip the saints for the work of ministry.

Ephesians 4:11-13 *He handed out gifts of apostle, prophet, evangelist, and pastor-teacher to train Christians in skilled servant work, working within Christ's body, the church, until we're all moving rhythmically and easily with each other, efficient and graceful in response to God's Son, fully mature adults, fully developed within and without, fully alive like Christ.*

Over the years we have seen the ministry of the local church evolve into more of a serving community and an equipping of the people to be a witness in the market place. We realize that the church is to be a house of prayer first where we get our orders from God, and also a school house that trains people for right living and being a witness of Christ in the marketplace and in whatever arena we find ourselves. Every one is placed in a particular sphere of influence to build the kingdom of God. The Kingdom is God's way of doing things which is the opposite of the world view. The Bible tells us we are saved by grace not works, but then we are to be doers or workers for Him. We are to make a difference, to be the salt and light in our sphere of influence.

God has been using us not only in our local church but in churches here in the US and the nations. Over the twenty-five years we have traveled on five continents to thirty-seven countries while flying over three million miles. These journeys have changed us and our perception of the world. We go because we have a heart for the leaders / ministers. A great number of them have not had the privilege or opportunity to go to Bible school, Seminary or even to be mentored into their calling. We have seen a great need among them to be fathered and for their wives to be mothered, and God is calling us to be those spiritual parents. We feel qualified to parent them since we bring to the table much experience: more than thirty years of full time ministry, more than forty years of marriage, and a wealth of education and experience. Fred has a bachelor's degree in business and a master of divinity degree along with much experience in the business field before answering the call to ministry; and I have a bachelor and a master of education degrees along with nineteen years of teaching school on the elementary, middle-school, and mostly high school levels. We both hold doctorates of ministry degrees and are ordained. Needless to say, we have spent a fortune on education even though the Veterans Administration provided for Fred's bachelor upon his discharge from the military, and a Pell grant provided for my bachelor of education in order to resume my teaching career in the USA. God does provide when we step out in faith to do what is necessary to fulfill our calling in life. God is always moved by faith. It is what pleases Him.

Hebrews 11:6 *And without faith it is impossible to please God,*

The thought of leaving our church and our family especially with the grandbabies in the picture now, was almost more than we could bear. Yet we knew God called us to minister to the world so we had to trust Him.

Matt 19: 29 NIV *And everyone who has left houses or brothers or sisters or father or mother or children or fields for my sake will receive a hundred times as much and will inherit eternal life.*

God has given us the grace and continues to do so. There is always a price to pay in serving Him. When He calls, He appoints and anoints to do the task at hand. But we must take up our cross and follow Him. We know without a shadow of doubt that it is God's will because we have received many confirmations. We are called to equip the nations. We've had a heart for different cultures and nations ever since we started. It began with our vision for Christ the Rock Church which we pioneered, a church with all kinds of people, a picture of Heaven on earth. We call it kingdom alignment because it is a picture of Heaven on earth. To have various cultures worshiping together was a miracle for Memphis Tennessee, a city divided along racial lines. God still does miracles today contrary to popular opinion.

Matthew 6:10 NIV *Your kingdom come, your will be done on earth as it is in heaven.*
1 Chronicles 16:12 *Remember the wonders he has done, his miracles …*
If God will do it in Memphis, He will do it anywhere,

Both Fred and I have always had a passion to right the injustice we see around us. I know that for myself as a young girl, I always took up for the underdog. I would befriend the strays and even into adulthood, I would find myself caring for women who needed 'something'. They were hurting, unhappy, mistreated, abused, and rejected. After fourteen years of being a French teacher, God called me to lay it down and become the women's pastor at the church. It was a difficult decision because I really loved my profession. It was my identity and it allowed me to experience my French heritage. I would pinch myself and say, "I am getting paid to do this! Wow!" Teaching was and is my passion. God blessed me with this talent. I have this desire to help people learn. As a teacher, I was considered a Master Teacher. Students came from the local universities to do their student teaching and training under my tutorship. Teaching was and is my God-given DNA.

When God wants to move us into another position He causes us to experience fatigue and weariness and become dissatisfied with where we are. That is what is called burn out. It's when we no longer have the grace to continue in that career, job or position. In other words we find ourselves in the wilderness because change is on the horizon. I call this phase of life 'divine discontentment'. God allows this to happen to us because He is preparing us for promotion. The Bible tells us He orders our steps and we are to walk in the steps He has prepared for us from the beginning of the world. We either believe His word or we don't. When this happens it is time to take inventory of our situation in life and ask ourselves if this is God transitioning us because He has something else for us to do or we simply need a vacation because we are tired. He has to get us to the place where we will do whatever it takes to get the relief we need in order to change – and that word 'change' is a bad word because nobody likes it. God did not mean for us to remain at the same station of life all of our days. He wants us to continue growing and we have become stagnant where we are, and it could be that we have finished the course there.

This also includes our church service or work. We get weary or we burn out because we are dealing with 'the same old same old' as the saying goes which means having to deal with the same people who have the same issues over and over again. God wants to move us on in order to war in a different zone because He knows we need a fresh new cause to contend with otherwise we would become exhausted. Even King David in the Bible was weary of fighting the same battles over and over again so God sent men to fight them for him so that he could go into the palace and be the CEO. You can read this in 2 Samuel 21. There is also something else at work here, if we do not move out of the way, then it prevents others from moving up into those positions. We have to make room for other heroes of faith to come forth.

I experienced that when God was calling me out of teaching. That last year was so tough. It was 1997, the year my sweet mother-in-law died, Chris got married and moved to Minneapolis, Denise went on the road with an evangelistic acting troupe, we became empty nesters and my heart was broken. Teaching French that year was totally exhausting and not fun anymore. I dreaded going to work every day and I did not understand what was happening. This was the job! I had no more grace for it and I did not understand what was happening to me. I had so enjoyed it that I would praise God for it when I would walk down the school halls and I would say to myself: "I get paid to do this". Wow! I thought I was losing control of my mind and my emotions. I needed to get a handle on things. The thought even crossed my mind that I perhaps needed counseling for depression. Then I began to realize that God was calling me out of my profession to be women's pastor at the church. I had not planned on retiring from teaching French, and becoming the women's pastor. It had never even appeared on my radar screen. I already was in the ministry along side my husband and I was already overseeing the women of the church. I had always felt I could do both. Why did I have to give up teaching? This also meant I would have to give up my salary which I really enjoyed, and my identity as Madame Bennett, the French Teacher. I was also mentoring teachers that were sent to me by the local universities. I had prestige. I was highly respected. However, God had other plans for me so He gave me such discontent that I had to obey Him in order to get relief. Once I accepted His plan for my life, a peace came upon me. I had finally entered His rest and I had stopped wrestling with Him. I had no idea what this call entailed but I was going to have to walk in faith and trust Him implicitly.

How interesting! God never opens a new door unless we close the old one. In other words, He never leads us into anything new unless we die to the former one. So I started showing up at church everyday 'to work' in my little office which was connected to Fred's. I had no idea what I was going to do and I missed my rigid teaching schedule. In fact I remember coming into Fred's office not long after I started, sitting in his counseling chair and weeping, and telling him that I had nothing to do. I added that giving up my teaching profession was the biggest mistake I had ever made and I was regretting it immensely.

Then God spoke to me and told me to be 'an ear' for a season by listening to the women He would bring to me for counseling rather than be 'a mouth' a teacher so to speak. So I started holding office hours at church and made myself available to the women of the church. I found myself 'counseling' women, which was really interesting since I have no training in that area, but I have the Holy Spirit who is the Counselor. I was showing them, sharing with them, and teaching them from the Bible the principles of God's word on how to be godly women, wives, and mothers; and to live victoriously rather than be victims of their circumstances.

Titus 2:4-5 NIV *Then they* (older women) *can train the younger women to love their husbands and children, 5 to be self-controlled and pure, to be busy at home, to be kind, and to be subject to their husbands, so that no one will malign the word of God.*

I was mentoring them and helping them get established in their God-given calling. I loved every minute of it because I was giving them life. I saw the light bulbs go on in their eyes and that was exhilarating for me. I did not realize it at the time but I was actually teaching in another setting 'one-on-one'. God was perfecting my teaching gift concerning the Scriptures since that was my counseling text from which I drew the principles for living. God was so good that He allowed me to do some teaching in Bible schools, church meetings, and retreats. He knew how much I enjoyed teaching but it was not my primary calling anymore. Once again, I was caring for the 'down and out' which is what God had called me to.

Luke 4:18 NIV *"The Spirit of the Lord is on me, because he has anointed me to preach good news to the poor. He has sent me to proclaim freedom for the prisoners and recovery of sight for the blind, to release the oppressed.*

This revelation concerning laying down my career came at our Women's Advance (we don't retreat, we advance) that took place the weekend Fred was on a mission trip to India. I was the preacher that Sunday morning so I informed our congregation what God had spoken to me and what had been confirmed through two sisters-in-Christ whom I respect, that I was to come beside my husband at the church and help carry the load. The people gave me a standing ovation. Apparently they had been praying for me to 'see the light' because they had seen me in this new position long before I did. Fred returned and I informed him what I had done. He was in agreement with me because God had already spoken to him while he was overseas. So I crossed the career bridge to the ministry bridge.

Fred and I realized that we would be together 24/7 because of the proximity of our offices, and we were going to have to adjust to this new way of life. We no longer had our own individual space. It was a time of dying to our individuality once again. Marriage always involves dying of the 'male ego' and the female 'woman's lib' mindsets:

'two deaths and one resurrection' as I heard one speaker say! We had to learn how to work together first in the office environment, and then God showed us how to flow together on the platform where we would share God's word and principles without one of us monopolizing all of the time which can be interesting since we both like to talk, both being mouths in the Kingdom of God. We had spoken individually at the same conferences / meetings / Bible colleges but had never shared the podium. God was preparing us to share the pulpit together because He was preparing us to be hosts for television. Nothing we do in life is for naught. God sees the big picture of our life and orchestrates the steps to get us there. That is why we can trust Him totally.

1 Cor 15:46 *The spiritual did not come first, but the natural, and after that the spiritual.* God always starts with the natural before going to the spiritual.
He created Adam before He brought forth the last Adam, Jesus. God is always transitioning us because He is always moving. We have to walk with Him like the children of Israel did by following His cloud in the daytime and the pillar of fire in the evening. We cannot get ahead of Him.

Fred and I have always detested injustice in whatever form it manifests. This is why God brought us together to cross the racial reconciliation bridge in Memphis. We are a perfect fit when it comes to reaching out to all kinds of people. He was brought up in church and saw the hypocrisy of racial prejudice. He has always had a passion for righteousness to prevail whether we were talking business, politics, education, the media or the ministry. He also has a passion to equip the Saints, and especially leaders for the work of the ministry. That is where his anointing lies now more than ever. He is a gifted speaker and has developed into a great one over time because of his spiritual DNA. Naturally, he is a good debater - he's always had the gift of gab and I know since I never win our arguments – ha! He says he can't believe he actually gets paid to preach. It is his passion. He would rather preach than do anything else.

We could hardly believe God had called us to pioneer and lead this great work, Christ the Rock Metro Church. We added 'Metro' once we were in our new worship center because we were reaching the entire Memphis metropolitan area. What was even more of a blessing to us was to see our children growing in their own ministry DNA. We were watching God develop them and make room for them in the ministry. It was truly a God-thing and not nepotism! Chris, our eldest son is married to a Canadian girl, Becky, (like father, like son) has served as the managing pastor and oversaw the men's ministry, the young adults (18-30 Somethings) and provided oversight for the care ministry at one time. God was establishing him by training him in all aspects of the ministry so that when the time came to be the senior pastor he would be ready. Becky who is the best daughter-in-law anyone could ask for, began overseeing 'Kinder-church' (5 and 6 year olds) along with the young moms fellowship. She is both beautiful on the inside as well as on the outside. She is the product of a Scottish mother and Sri Lankan father. Chris and Becky have three beautiful children, two daughters, Maia 8 and Claire 3, and a son, Levi 6. Grandchildren are and have been rich blessings in our lives. They keep us smiling and keep us young. They are our reward for having had children.

Our daughter Denise has grown into a wonderful student pastor with a strong relevant preaching/teaching gift, and her husband Jeremy is a gifted musician and song writer who is our praise and worship leader whom she assists. They both share in each others callings and ministries which makes them an effective team. They also oversee the young adult ministry, the college age group of people. We are so blessed to have them along side us.

Our two older grandchildren, Maia and Levi have already begun to declare what they are going to be when they grow up. Maia says she is going to be a teacher and Levi says he is going to be a praise and worship leader like his uncle Jeremy. What a blessing! We are looking forward to seeing how God will work in Claire, Judah and Liam.

This is where we are as a family. God has chosen, called, and equipped each one of us to do the work of the ministry. It is not nepotism either. It is God's way. Posterity! We see it with Abraham, Isaac and Jacob. All we have to do is submit to Him and allow Him to flow through us. There is nothing like serving God and the body of Christ with the spiritual gifts and talents He has blessed us with. That is where we find our total fulfillment and our joy is made full.

We were disappointed to realize that the people who were with us did not agree with the word that God calls families. They saw the writing on the wall that Chris was going to inherit the ministry one day and they were against this idea. This is when the church began to shake.

Gen 17:7 NIV *I will establish my covenant as an everlasting covenant between me and you and your descendants after you for the generations to come, to be your God and the God of your descendants after you.*

CHAPTER 11

THE TRANSITION BRIDGE
SHAKE RATTLE AND ROLL

"One last shaking, from top to bottom, stem to stern."
The phrase "one last shaking" means a thorough
housecleaning, getting rid of all the historical and
religious junk so that the unshakable
essentials stand clear and uncluttered.

Hebrews 12:26-27

S ince the day after Christmas 2005, called Boxing Day in English influenced cultures, we have been in corporate prayer at Christ the Rock Metro Church in Memphis, Tennessee. After nearly thirty years of ministry, 2005 was one of the most challenging years we had ever faced. It was as if the momentum which had carried us from our earliest days of ministry had abated and we were adrift, threatened with shipwreck. If you would like to know more about our history as ministers of the Gospel and that of our church prior to 2002, please reference Valerie's book, "Christ the Rock Metro Church, Our Story" which is available for purchase on the web site. www.christtherockmemphis.org

But this book is about more than our personal history, it is intended to help anyone who is transitioning from one phase of life and ministry to another. Transitions can be draining, difficult and dangerous but with God's help we can do all things through Christ who strengthens us! He wants us to "crossover" into the next dimension of the kingdom come on the earth! I am calling it a "New Kingdom Day."

Our ministry was birthed in the Charismatic Movement of the 1960's and 70's. It was a glorious wave of God's refreshing which carried us from lay ministry in our home church; to ministering in a rural United Methodist Church which grew from thirty-five to three hundred and fifty people in five years; to the founding and growing of Christ the Rock Metro Church. The Charismatic Movement was about a spiritual awakening, a renewal in the mainline Protestant and Catholic Churches. We witnessed firsthand the fruit of this movement in the suburban church where we were members; in a rural church where I served as a student pastor; and in the church we founded which draws from urban and suburban areas.

In the fall of 2002 it appeared that we had arrived! The church had grown to a membership in excess of two thousand. We had completed construction of a beautiful three thousand seat sanctuary. The annual income of the church surpassed three million dollars. According to the vision, the congregation had become increasingly multiethnic. We were traveling the world in ministry. Our children, both natural and spiritual, were rising up to take their place in ministry with us. The hand of the Lord was upon us and we were looking forward to an even more glorious future. But a not so funny thing happened on the way to our glorious future. One year and a half after entering the new Worship Center we realized the honeymoon was over. We began to hear a lot of murmuring.

Romans 16:17-18 NIV *I urge you brothers, to watch out for those who cause divisions and put obstacle in your way that are contrary to the teaching you have learned. Keep away from them. For such people are not serving our Lord Christ, but their own appetites. By smooth talk and flattery they deceive the minds of naïve people.*

Val and I began to realize that some of the people were discontented and even resented the new worship center. What's more, they did not want to pay for it either so the battle for financial stability began. Up until this point finances had never been a divisive issue in this ministry. On top of this we were contending with a spirit of competition and contention in the leadership which was having a negative affect on the unity of the congregation. It felt like the vision was being high-jacked or sabotaged and it saddened us. There was spiritual warfare going on within the walls of the church. We know that every church has its issues because where ever there are people, there will be drama. So at first we thought we were simply learning to adjust to a new bigger sanctuary and the growing pains that go along with it. We soon understood that this was not the case. Disunity was increasing. We were going to have to make some drastic changes.

Not being confrontational by nature I delayed taking drastic measures as long as I could but it only made matters worse. I was trying to lead by example rather than harshly ruling over some of the people. I've always sought to think the best and to give people the benefit of the doubt. In hindsight I erred by being too lenient with some people, especially those in leadership.

Val and I desperately needed God's direction otherwise this ship was going to run aground or sink. Talk about a sense of foreboding! We thought about all the one hundred plus people on staff who relied upon the church for their livelihood. And among that number were many of our own family members! We finally came to the place where we were determined to do whatever was necessary, no matter the cost. Our heart was set on doing whatever God required so this ministry could continue. We believed in our heart of hearts that God birthed it so it was His baby and He would continue to care for it by directing our steps.

Prior to the shaking, Val and I took a group from our church on a mission's trip to Zambia along with our good friend Craig Strickland, Senior Pastor of Hope Church here in this city, to do a leadership conference in the fall of 2004. Sitting in the Johannesburg, South Africa airport on our way home, we were reflecting on our trip. We had also been talking about the drama we were experiencing at our church. I had been reading a book Craig had recommended, entitled, "Good to Great." It is actually a business book but is written by a Christian. Since I held a degree in Business Administration and had been in business it was not difficult for me to profit from this kind of material. It compelled me to make some very difficult decisions because our church growth had leveled off. There were stress fractures in our leadership and it was obvious that Christ the Rock Metro Church was "structurally deficient!" We had built a beautiful, state of the art, earthquake resistant sanctuary, but the leadership structure was deficient and could not support the growth God wanted to give us.

Val had a dream prior to this trip and in it she saw how our church had become like a mall with every ministry functioning as an independent enterprise from one another without any regard for the vision God had given us for the whole church. There was 'di-vision' (more than one vision) among the leadership and they were constantly vying for the same people causing much confusion and disunity. The people did not know whom to follow or obey because of all the rumors they were hearing. It is like what Paul was telling the Corinthians.

1 Cor 1:12 *Some of you are saying, "I am a follower of Paul"; and others say that they are for Apollos or for Peter; and some that they alone are the true followers of Christ.*

We knew some of the leaders had ministry aspirations of their own but right then was not the time to be voicing them. It was the manifestation of an "Absalom" spirit. King David's son Absalom had his own aspirations to be a leader so he drew men's hearts to himself away from his father's leadership thus causing much division and confusion among the people. This tactic was intended to take the Kingdom away from King David.

2 Sam 15:5-6 *Also, whenever anyone approached him to bow down before him, Absalom would reach out his hand, take hold of him and kiss him. 6 Absalom behaved in this way toward all the Israelites who came to the king asking for justice, and so he stole the hearts of the men of Israel.* NIV

A possible church split was looming on the horizon. All of this turmoil was clogging up the flow of ministry and it caused the people to withdraw from serving and tithing. We were feeling the pressure and with much wrestling, I made an extremely difficult business decision by cutting in half the salaries of the top tier leadership including myself in order to alleviate some of the burden which would take effect beginning in 2005. Our administrator had already made some staff changes but it still wasn't enough. It was also time for these leaders to start moving towards their own ministries because they had their own dreams that needed to be fulfilled. I was having to act like a mother bird and gradually push her birds out of the nest so that they could learn to fly solo. They had gotten too comfortable. In hindsight, it was God getting our attention so that we would make the necessary changes in order to reach this new culture that was up and coming. At this point, the ship began to shake rattle and roll!

Heb 12:26-27 NIV *At that time his voice shook the earth, but now he has promised, "Once more I will shake not only the earth but also the heavens." 27 The words "once more" indicate the removing of what can be shaken — that is, created things — so that what cannot be shaken may remain.*

Tumultuous times like these will bring God's people to their knees and that is exactly the effect it had on us. We began to cry out to the Lord as we mentioned, on Boxing Day, for His presence and help concerning our ministry and the church. Looking back, we can see that the day was a prophetic sign to us, to let us know what God was doing in our lives and ministry. He wanted us to get out of the "box," the box being our comfort zone, our mindset, our ways and understanding, and to a certain extent, even our history. Quite simply the Lord was calling us to come into line with what He was doing in this new generation. He is all about growing His kingdom on this earth. His word never changes but His methods do. What had worked before to reach the people was no longer effective.

Storm clouds began to gather and we found ourselves in a fight for our ministry and church. What we thought would give the people reasons to rejoice with us, caused many of them to reject our leadership and leave. We had taught for years that the real test of any ministry was its ability to pass on to the next generation what God had given them. Yet we found ourselves in a storm of transition that threatened to sink the boat and destroy everything we had spent our Christian lives building.

We felt abandoned by our long time friends and experienced a depth of loneliness and despair we had never encountered before. It made us totally dependent on the Lord and He became our all sufficiency. We could not be entangled with anyone or anything. Ties had to be severed! We needed to be free because God was orchestrating our future behind the scenes. It was during this dire time that the Lord in His mercy and grace brought Mervyn and Muriel Mediwake, our dear dear friends from Lethbridge, to Memphis. They thought they were on an assignment from God to be with Chris and Becky and help them as they transitioned into the leadership of CTR. Little did we know! God had relocated them here to be with us. They stood with us and prayed with and for us. They also encouraged us and believed God with us for His outcome. We prayed together with a few faithful morning and night for two years until they were called back to Toronto to be with their daughter, Anne Marie, who was expecting triplets. Prayer is what got us through the two most tumultuous years of shaking at CTR, otherwise we would have died of broken hearts. We experienced a small measure of what Jesus went through in the garden of Gethsemane where His destiny to die on a cross for all mankind was settled once and for all. For us the die was cast, we had to move on with what God had for us not knowing what that was yet. We had to die to the ministry of Christ The Rock Church. God was going to use us to build a bridge beyond that of pastors of the local church to pastors of the body at large.

Matthew 26:39 *Going a little ahead, he fell on his face, praying, "My Father, if there is any way, get me out of this. But please, not what I want. You, what do you want?"*
Matthew 26:42 *Again he prayed, "My Father, if there is no other way than this, drinking this cup to the dregs, I'm ready. Do it your way."*

I was watching the movie "Castaway" recently. The star, Tom Hanks, is "air-shipwrecked" and marooned on a deserted island. Hanks plays the part of Chuck Noland, an engaged, workaholic Federal Express inspector, who travels around the world testing the effectiveness of international shipping offices. His frenetic schedule puts a strain on his relationship with longtime girlfriend Helen. But when a plane crash leaves him stranded and isolated from all other human beings on a remote Pacific island for four years, Chuck slowly becomes transformed both mentally and physically as he struggles to survive.

You see, it is in transition times like these that we must be transformed or die! The death is not necessarily a sudden execution, or a drop dead experience, but is usually a long, slow fading into extinction. This is why it is so important to know what day we are living in! There are days of salvation, days of restoration, days of reformation, days of emancipation and even days of judgment. But I believe that we are living in a day of transformation. After 40 years of experiencing the transforming power of God's word, we are now being called into a kingdom time where we will be used of God to transform our world.

In one scene from the Castaway, the ubiquitous FedEx boxes begin to wash ashore from the wrecked jet and "Chuck," Tom Hanks, begins to open them looking for something useful. He finds things which are of little value to a man stranded on a tropical island. The boxes are full of things like ice skates, a volley ball, video tapes, and a prom dress. But when all is said and done he finds a use for it all. What's the old saying? "Necessity is the mother of invention!" New things and new ways are like this. We become so dependent on our old ways that it is hard to imagine how we can get along without them. But once we are stripped of them we find use for new things. You could say that the marooned Chuck had to "get out of the box" in order to survive; to escape the island which was his prison; and to return to his home and life. But as Tom Hanks discovers in this movie, you can go back home, back to the familiar, but things will have changed.

Tragically, Tom Hanks' character had no apparent relationship with God. He was so alone on that island that he resorted to fellowshipping with a volley ball upon which he painted a face. His imaginary friend, named "Wilson," helped him to keep from going crazy. It was a modern version of a "graven image" substitute for God. Of course people do this all the time. We expect friends or spouses or children or even "successful" ministers to substitute for a relationship with God. Thankfully, our God is not merely an impersonal "higher power" but a friend who will never leave us or forsake us. For those who believe, God really is our strength.

Psalm 46:1 NIV *God is our refuge and strength, an ever-present help in trouble.*

In the wildly popular TV series "Friends," friendship really is like a volleyball batted back and forth as people try and score points with or on one another. As is so often the case in the NY-Hollywood media axis, the values presented are at odds with the values expressed in the Bible and with Judeo-Christian culture. The word of God reveals that friends are not just a plaything to amuse us for a season until we grow weary of them.

True friends are those who will speak the truth to us in love without judging us. It is a two way street! Have we shown ourselves to be a friend indeed? There is a principle in the Bible about reaping what we have sown. To have friends, one must be friendly to others.

Proverbs 27:6 NKJV *"Faithful are the wounds of a friend, But the kisses of an enemy are deceitful.*
Proverbs 18:24 NKJV *"A man who has friends must himself be friendly, But there is a friend who sticks closer than a brother*

"There is no wilderness like a life without friends."
Baltasar Gracian y Morales

When I began to preach on friendship in 2005, I was shocked by the backlash. I was accused of being too evangelistic. I believe God called us to reach out to the lost in order to expand His Kingdom. Too many wanted church to just be about what they could get out of it for themselves. I was ministering on how through just being friendly we can break through many of the barriers which separate us. Jesus was proactive in befriending people so that he could get around their resistance to the gospel of the kingdom. Jesus often asked such people to give Him something, which is a pretty novel approach to the lost. He asked Simon for the use of his boat as a pulpit. He asked the Samaritan woman for a drink. He asked Zacchaeus for something to eat. Jesus often befriended people whom others had little use for. He was friendly to them and they would respond to Him.

There are times and seasons when we all feel like sailors caught in storms, sometimes shipwrecked and in need of friends. We are like everyone else who is just trying to hold on, but finding out that the things which had worked for us before are of no use to us now. Now we have to find a new way forward. As every month seems to be marked by another fallen ministry star, I am saddened and dismayed. But I must also confess to a certain amount of fear. It is a fear that I might also after all these years fall short of the glory of God and bring shame to the name I bear. It is the fear of God which keeps us but has been largely ignored for some time now.

Tragically, many in our movement are in denial that anything is intrinsically wrong. But I am convinced that every falling star is a signal that we should be examining ourselves both individually and corporately. I love the Charismatic movement, which has been my life for the past 33 years, but something is terribly wrong! I fear that like so many who have gone before us we have begun to substitute lying signs and wonders for real Pentecostal power, and personality for true godly character.

Revelation 8:10 *The third Angel trumpeted. A huge Star, blazing like a torch, fell from Heaven, wiping out a third of the rivers and a third of the springs.*

The water which was once so pure, so sweet and so full of life is being made bitter by those without a healthy fear of God. These fallen stars still have many followers and supporters. They say that it doesn't matter what they do so long as their ministries are accompanied by signs and wonders. It is the problem of being so enamored with the gift that we discount the fruit. Jesus said that we would know the tree by the fruit it bears and not by the shadow it casts!

2 Thessalonians 2:9-12 *The Anarchist's coming is all Satan's work. All his power and signs and miracles are fake, evil sleight of hand that plays to the gallery of those who hate the truth that could save them. And since they're so obsessed with evil, God rubs their noses in it — gives them what they want. Since they refuse to trust truth, they're banished to their chosen world of lies and illusions.*

Even Pharaoh's magicians had power and were able to conjure up some signs and wonders of their own which gave Pharaoh and the Egyptians a false sense of confidence! Satan has some power and is able to work signs but they are "lying wonders." That is, the signs and wonders do not point to the truth. Their effect is to distract and confuse. Up to a point it seemed that the Egyptian gods were just as strong as the God of the Hebrews. But the signs performed by God through Moses pointed to the real deal. We must be able to discern the difference. When we see the unbelieving prospering and their agenda seeming to prevail in the land, we must not lose heart. And we must not fall into the trap of thinking that all signs are "lying wonders," for to do so robs the church of its power and makes it impossible to receive the kingdom of God on the earth.

I am concerned about so-called signs of the kingdom which are of little or no consequence. In the name of Jesus demons tremble; blind eyes are opened; the lame walk; the lepers are cleansed; and even the dead are raised! Let us not substitute the pitiful and profane for the powerful and prophetic!

Hebrews 2:1-4 *It's crucial that we keep a firm grip on what we've heard so that we don't drift off. If the old message delivered by the angels was valid and nobody got away with anything, do you think we can risk neglecting this latest message, this magnificent salvation? First of all, it was delivered in person by the Master, then accurately passed on to us by those who heard it from him. All the while God was validating it with gifts through the Holy Spirit, all sorts of signs and miracles, as he saw fit.*

As we came to the end of this forty year period, 1967-2007, Republican Senator Charles Grassley, Illinois, had initiated an investigation into what he and others considered the excessive and lavish lifestyles of certain ministers. Most of those targeted by the investigation were associated with the preaching of the "prosperity gospel."

The temptations of the gold, the glory and the girls, or in some cases, the boys, were bringing down many!

1 Timothy 6:3-10 *If you have leaders there who teach otherwise, who refuse the solid words of our Master Jesus and this godly instruction tag them for what they are: ignorant windbags who infect the air with germs of envy, controversy, bad-mouthing, suspicious rumors. Eventually there's an epidemic of backstabbing, and truth is but a distant memory. They think religion is a way to make a fast buck. A devout life does bring wealth, but it's the rich simplicity of being yourself before God. Since we entered the world penniless and will leave it penniless, if we have bread on the table and shoes on our feet, that's enough. But if it's only money these leaders are after, they'll self-destruct in no time. Lust for money brings trouble and nothing but trouble. Going down that path, some lose their footing in the faith completely and live to regret it bitterly ever after.*

I have no problem with teaching prosperity so long as it is not confused with the love of money. From the above scripture it appears that the difference between Biblical prosperity and the love of money is contentment. The prosperity we should be interested in is that which resources the work of the Lord. It is not about gaining wealth so that we can lavish it upon ourselves. All true doctrines and teachings will accord, be in agreement with and lead to godliness. Which is it to be? Are we to be lovers of pleasure or lovers of God? Prosperity appears to be more of a byproduct than a goal in the New Testament. The prosperity our family has enjoyed has come upon us gradually, through the years as we were faithful to obey and trust God in all things. It was not the desire to get rich which motivated our giving and tithing, but the desire to see the kingdom come on the earth.

God calls us to live according to His word and not adopt the world system.

2 Timothy 3:1-5 NIV *But mark this: There will be terrible times in the last days. People will be lovers of themselves, lovers of money, boastful, proud, abusive, disobedient to their parents, ungrateful, unholy, without love, unforgiving, slanderous, without self-control, brutal, not lovers of the good, treacherous, rash, conceited, lovers of pleasure rather than lovers of God—having a form of godliness but denying its power. Have nothing to do with them.*

Concerning "the form of godliness", I have always heard that this is referring to people who deny Pentecostal power which manifests in signs and wonders. But I have come to realize that it is talking about something else. Verses 2-4 describe the kind of people that I did not want to be like in the world. But when it is qualified by verse 5 it aptly describes what many in the church have become.

Therefore it would seem that every forty years the church needs a thorough housecleaning, much like Jesus did in the temple when He purged those more interested in money than prayer!

Matthew 21:12-13 *Jesus went straight to the Temple and threw out everyone who had set up shop, buying and selling. He kicked over the tables of loan sharks and the stalls of dove merchants. He quoted this text: My house was designated a house of prayer; You have made it a hangout for thieves.*

The Charismatic movement is now over forty years old and we are beginning to witness the decline of its influence. Some have declared that it is over and it is dead. Perhaps the more accurate term is in decline. In any case, the Charismatic Renewal started as a response to a dry and thirsty people who wanted to know the reality of God's presence. We wanted to find again the living waters which would cause us to never thirst again. Charismatics are often criticized for being too experience oriented but that is precisely what was missing in much of the church.

I believe that we stand at the threshold of a new move of God. Once again God's people are thirsty for the Spirit. Their inner life is dry and barren and it is time to simplify and to clarify! The Lord spoke this word to us in prayer during the summer of 2007. We had just returned from the "The Call" in Nashville and were seeking God on how to prepare for 2008 and beyond. I think it remains to be seen if the great praise and prayer meeting attended by approximately seventy thousand people was the end or the beginning of a move of God. Perhaps it was both! Yet so much of what we witnessed seemed to be rooted in the last forty years.

As in the days of Elijah there are most certainly other altars. Not coincidentally, on 7 / 7 / 7 altars were built on every continent at the behest of former Vice President and Nobel Prize winner Al Gore. Just as in Nashville, football stadiums were used as venues and filled with rock music. The speeches warned of the impending doom caused by Global Warming. This issue has become the next great showdown with the scientific community.

As I mentioned in the prologue of this book, I purposely use the term "structurally deficient" because on August 1st, 2007, forty years after it was built, the I-35W bridge that connected the twin cities of Minneapolis and St. Paul, Minnesota, collapsed into the Mississippi River. It was revealed that the bridge had been judged structurally deficient several years ago and at the time of collapse was under superficial repair. I did not want this fate to befall the ministry we have spent our Christian lives building and intended to pass on to the next generation. Too often in life and ministry we think that structural deficiencies can be dealt with by resurfacing. But the resurfacing, as with this bridge, may actually contribute to its failure.

Not coincidentally, the mission declaration of our ministry is "building bridges together." From the very beginning of our ministry thirty years ago we've been building bridges wherever there was a gap. We've built bridges between generations, denominations, races, nations and between the church and the un-churched. But I have been asking the Lord if this ministry needed a new, updated statement? The answer came with a sudden resounding boom when the I-35W bridge suddenly shook and fell into the Mississippi River! I was reminded of how important it is to build (and maintain) bridges that last. When bridges fail or are destroyed people are injured and killed, and in this case, the life of two cities, Minneapolis and St. Paul, would be disrupted for many months to come.

It is another sign of the times that this bridge was constructed 40 years ago and was due to be replaced because of "structural deficiencies! If we have ears to hear, and eyes that see, the Lord is telling us that unreliable bridges, as well as unreliable leaders and unreliable relationships, will prevent us from crossing over into the next phase of His kingdom come on the earth. If it's shaky because of structural deficiencies it isn't a good escape route! GET THE GUANO OUT! Forgive my crudeness but in order to get some people's attention, especially ordained ministers of the Gospel, it is often necessary to shock them! It may be many years before it is finally determined what brought that Minnesota bridge down but at least one contributing factor has been uncovered. It seems that there was an area where the steel beams were fitted together that was a nesting place for pigeons and rats. The junction was covered by a steel plate on two sides forming a type of box. The access hole at the bottom was to be used by inspectors so they could make periodic inspections. The problem was that the inspectors were reluctant to stick their head, and only their head into this aperture because of the resident vermin and their prodigious deposits of guano!

What is my point? It seems that this collected guano when mixed with water produces an acid that slowly eats away at the steel. Probably not enough to bring a steel and concrete bridge down, but enough to further weaken the structure. I'm suggesting that this has a spiritual application in our lives and ministries. When we fail to deal with the "guano" in our hidden places; secret sins in our hearts and minds; in our relationships; in our ministries, it may not have an immediate or visible effect. But with the passage of time and further accumulation, these dark places can become breeding grounds of sickness and disease. The only way I have found to look into these horrible, frightening and disgusting places is through Holy Spirit anointed prayer.

Since the day we began to pray in earnest for the Lord's presence and to spend time in His face, He has graciously been ministering to us. In 2006 we surrendered control of all the ministry to Him and prayed morning and evening with a few faithful intercessors. We dedicated ourselves to the proposition that if the Lord didn't initiate and anoint it, we weren't going to continue with it! We put everything we had been doing on the altar and asked our God who is a consuming fire to consume whatever He was no longer doing. It is at the altar of God that we are altered.

We had also asked Him to show us what He was doing that we were not, so that we could get involved with what He was doing. This had precipitated changes in the way we did things as well as in the way we thought about things. Prayer had become the birthing place of all we tried to do in the name of the Lord. Hebrews 12:29 NIV *for our "God is a consuming fire".*
Psalm 43:4 NIV *Then will I go to the altar of God, to God, my joy and my delight.*

When our new sanctuary was under construction I noticed a large space had been designated for storage overlooking the sanctuary. At first I requested and then had to fight for the space to be converted into a prayer room. In those days fighting for even the simplest changes was common. It should have been a storm warning for us! I called it our Upper Room at the time. Until Boxing Day 2005 it was under utilized and often frequented by people who were praying independently or in groups which had their own agenda. There were and still are some intercessors that have been very faithful to the church's vision. I thank God that He compelled me to finish that storage space as a prayer room. It has been our place of refuge, refreshing and rebirth! Our prayer room had become a womb of the Spirit.

Over the years we have come to the conclusion that many things can be delegated to others but the leadership of the prayer ministry of the church is not one of them. And one of the very hard lessons we learned over the years was that leaders who would not pray with you, were probably not with you!

There were many aspects of ministry which demanded our time, but leaders should give themselves first and foremost to prayer and to the ministry of the word.

Acts 6:2-3 NIV *So the Twelve gathered all the disciples together and said, "It would not be right for us to neglect the ministry of the word of God in order to wait on tables. Brothers, choose seven men from among you who are known to be full of the Spirit and wisdom. We will turn this responsibility over to them and will give our attention to prayer and the ministry of the word."*

We are convinced by the word of God, by experience, and by observation that leaders must pray together to maximize their effectiveness and avoid shipwreck. If we are going to "build bridges together" we must come into kingdom alignment. Praying our way into kingdom alignment means we stop asking God to bless what we've thought to do, or even what He blessed in the past and then we begin to ask God to show us what He is doing today. When Jesus' disciples observed that the miraculous works He did came after times of prayer, they asked Him to teach them how to pray. It was then that Jesus taught them what we call the Lord's Prayer found in the Gospel of Matthew. I want to stress Matt 6:10: *your kingdom come, your will be done on earth as it is in heaven. NIV* A more appropriate interpretation might be to pray for God to establish His kingship, His rule, and His authority in our lives while on the earth. We need His plans and His purposes to be accomplished in us and through us on the earth.

In the Garden of Gethsemane, just before Jesus is about to hand over the kingdom to His disciples, He exhorts them to pray with Him.

Matthew 26:40-41 NIV *Then he returned to his disciples and found them sleeping. "Could you men not keep watch with me for one hour?" he asked Peter. "Watch and pray so that you will not fall into temptation. The spirit is willing, but the body is weak."*

If we will not "watch and pray" together as leaders, then we will enter into temptation. Matthew 6:13 NIV *And lead us not into temptation, but deliver us from the evil one.'* The devil will tempt us to work in our natural might and in the power of the flesh. We'll begin to betray one another; to argue about who is the greatest among us; to run away in the face of opposition; and even to deny one another. These are all temptations that Jesus' disciples faced and failed because they had not learned how to come together in prayer. There was no structural integrity upon which to build a bridge that would enable them to crossover to a new kingdom age. They would have to die to themselves and how things had been and be birthed anew as Jesus' church.

Matthew 16:18-20 NIV *And I tell you that you are Peter, and on this rock I will build my church, and the gates of Hades will not overcome it. I will give you the keys of the kingdom of heaven; whatever you bind on earth will be bound in heaven, and whatever you loose on earth will be loosed in heaven." Then he warned his* disciples *not to tell anyone that he was the Christ.*

You see it wasn't time yet for that revelation to be released to the general public. The revelation of Jesus as the Christ would be given to and through His church. It was only after 50 days of prayer and fasting together they were able to crossover from the days of John the Baptist to the dawning of the kingdom age come on the earth. The Day of Pentecost was the fruit of a turnaround for them. Our friend James Goll teaches that every new move of God has a sound; a manifestation; and a revelation. There is a continuing, progressive revelation which we can only receive through prayer and fasting in God's timing.

Kingdom Alignment is not only about our ministries and our relationships. It is also about our inward, spiritual life. As we are approaching the end of 2007, I (Fred) sensed the Lord was dealing with us ever more strongly in this regard. He wanted us to not only put our ministry on the altar but also ourselves. As we know it is on the altar we are altered. I know that fasting is usually associated with food and drink or bad habits but I sensed the Spirit was calling us to the "Simple Life." No, I'm not talking about Paris Hilton and Nicole Richey's absurd TV program! Or maybe I am! What they parody, which is of course the opposite lifestyle, is more conducive to the things of the Spirit. The Holy Spirit is calling us, compelling us to come into a kind of wilderness before we cross over into this new "kingdom kairos." The wilderness is a time of preparation for promotion. Things which were once a help to our spirituality may have become an unnecessary crutch which is slowing us down. Practices which were once good and drew our attention to the Lord may now be a distraction. I think that for some, perhaps not all, this could be true of dancing, banner waving, and other dramatic expressions of worship which are more Old Testament based than New. Please hear my heart. I've practiced all these things in worship. So I'm not trashing or bashing these practices or their practitioners, but I do believe the Lord is calling on us to "Simplify" for a season. As the song so beautifully says, "come back to the heart of worship." He wants us to appreciate communion with Him again in the pure and simple beauty of holiness before we learned these other things. We don't have to copy the ancient Israelites or the ponderously liturgical in order to draw near to God. So much of what they did and do is more of a substitute for the simplicity of the purely spiritual. It so easily becomes a form of godliness while denying its power.

CHAPTER 12

THE TRANSFER BRIDGE
PASSING THE BATON

Don't you see that children are God's best gift?
the fruit of the womb his generous legacy?

Ps 127:3

On December 6, 2006, Kent Christmas who is a dear friend and a prophetic gift shared a word with our church Sunday morning concerning the rough time we had gone through over the past three years. The gist of it was that He wanted the arm of the flesh to be gone and the simplicity of faith returned. That was 'the sweet' God was bringing back and it was very comforting. He also spoke to Chris.

Here is the gist and I quote: There is a mantle of the Lord upon you. I don't know your name but I know you're the Pastor's son. God said there is a spirit of preaching upon you. God said you are going to rattle the gates of hell by what the Lord has done in your spirit. God has made you a man of faith. God said I'm raising you up as a new generation. There will come a day that the mantle of this church is going to be upon you and He is preparing you for that hour. And do not be moved when it comes for the Lord said that I am doing a deep thing in you that when I give you the responsibility you will not be lifted up in pride, even in the shifting and changes that are going on in your spirit. You wonder sometimes- Lord am I capable? The Lord said it's never going to be your strength or your ability or your knowledge or your talent. It is because you have a servant's heart and you are not full of ambition. The Lord said I am going to use you to lead this place in depths that you have not known.

I am paraphrasing what Kent told Fred. He said that as a father, he had to stay close to the house in order to thwart any attack the enemy might try on Christ the Rock Church because of its vulnerability in the midst of transition. He also told us that God was severing our friends because they were only interested in the ministry for what they could get out of it and that they did not want to embrace what God was doing at that point. This answered our questions as to why they jumped ship and abandoned us in the middle of the shaking. It was heart wrenching because some of these same people had begun with us and others had been with us in excess of 20 years. We had come to the conclusion that we had to rely totally on God and not people. That was a very hard and painful lesson to learn.

So here we are, 2007 and the transition was slowly progressing in our church. The waters had calmed down enough to where we were beginning to feel as though we were entering a place called Fair Haven spiritually.
Acts 27:8 NIV *We moved along the coast with difficulty and came to a place called Fair Havens,*

We were still praying every morning diligently and sensing God was preparing us for a new day which also meant He was completing the old one at Christ the Rock. The 7 of 2007 means completion. What God was doing was so fresh and sweet to our souls. It felt as though we were retuning to our first love which was so pure and innocent. He was simplifying our lives because we had picked up a lot of excess baggage on this Christian journey. Fred was preaching less and Chris was preaching more. Fred was slowly delegating more of the responsibilities of the ministry to Chris and backing somewhat out of the picture in order to find his niche. We began to feel the burden of the ministry lift because we had carried it practically alone for almost 25 years.

In October 2007, our son Chris was installed as the senior pastor of Christ The Rock Church. It was an emotional morning for me but it was wonderful and I believe the will of God. The congregation has known for several years that this day would come. By doing it now and not waiting until I retired or died, I felt that it would make a greater prophetic statement. Dr. Craig Strickland from Hope Presbyterian Church and Pastor Gary Faulkner from Cummings Street Baptist Church joined me in laying hands on Chris. I introduced what we were doing and then Dr. Craig and Pastor Gary shared a word of commissioning. I then asked the congregation to extend their hand of blessing and it was done. Val also passed the baton of 'first lady' to Becky.

I believe that what was done stands in stark contrast to what we usually see and certainly what we have witnessed lately in Memphis, Tennessee. Countless people have testified that they had never witnessed anything like this before. Usually a congregation is left to figure it out for themselves or some third party in a denomination steps in and appoints the next pastor. What we were trying to model is the passing of a mantle from one generation to another. We are standing in faith on the promise of Deuteronomy 1, that if the Lord can get it to three consecutive generations, He can and will get it to a thousand. This is why He calls Himself the God of Abraham, Isaac and Jacob. Jacob accepted God's destiny for his life, his name was changed to that of a nation, Israel.

Elijah left the mantle to Elisha but only when he died and then he left it on the ground. One way to read the narrative is to hear Elijah's reluctance to give Elisha the mantle. Ever since the cave where Elijah was rebuked by the Lord, he had been reticent to fully do the will of the Lord. He had placed the mantle on Elisha when he found him plowing in the field but he is unwilling to do it in the sight of others. So God's will was done regardless.

It was a process that began when he moved back home the end of December of 2000 with his wife Becky and their new born baby Maia at the time. He was not a novice but well trained in all aspects of the ministry. He had already been in full time ministry seven years. His mother and I knew this was God's will and timing for our son to take over. For the last two years prior to this changing of the guard, we had found the ministry extremely difficult because we no longer had the grace to be the pastors anymore. It was God doing His thing again!

For me, it had been a time of wrestling over when to pass the baton. I was totally burned out after having gone through the turmoil of the last three years which was part of the God-ordained transition. He was changing our mantles of authority because He had other plans for us. We faced an identity crisis. We had been the founders and senior pastors for twenty-five years of Christ The Rock Church. And now to no longer be the pastors, it felt really strange. It was more of an adjustment for me than it was for Val because she had already transitioned from her teaching job to become the women's pastor whereas I had been the senior pastor of two churches for a total of thirty years. Val continued to be the women's pastor and I no longer knew where I fit in at Christ The Rock Church. I had been serving Pastor Craig Strickland at Hope Church overseeing the Church Developers Network for the last year, which is a monthly meeting for surrounding pastors and leaders on church growth and fellowship, and acted as a consultant for many of the pastors in the city and suburbs. God was using me locally and globally. In essence I was being used as an Apostle to the Church at large. I was enjoying this new role.

It was a bitter sweet time. I say sweet because as soon as the reins of leadership were placed in Chris' hands, a new authority came upon him and he began to draw new younger people. He is an excellent teacher/ preacher and very relevant to this new generation. The bitter part was that some of the older people who had started with us resented Chris becoming the pastor. It is Biblical to pass the baton to the next generation in the family if they have the goods which Chris did. We are proud of our children because they have turned out to be godly people who love God, live for Him and want to serve Him. They chose of their own volition to be in the ministry. They decided to go this route because they were reared on the Bible instead of Doctor Spock's book. Our children are the second generation to serve Him in ministry and we believe and are declaring our grandchildren will continue.

Josh 24:15 NIV *But as for me and my household, we will serve the Lord."*

Job 22:28 NKJV *You will also declare a thing, And it will be established for you;*

Because of our promotion beyond the local church, our children are now the leaders of Christ The Rock Church. What we see happening today in our church is what we saw happen twenty-five years ago when we planted this church. Lots of young families with lots of small children are pouring in! It is a sign of new life! It is a breath of fresh air for us seasoned folk! God had to prune Christ The Rock Church in order to bring forth this new growth. We are seeing whole families transformed by God's power because they are following Christ's teachings. We have absolutely no regrets because it was God's plan before the foundation of the world. We are praising God that the vision continues. It has the same core values:

Racial Healing / Diversity
Spirit Filled
Friendly / Relevant
Life Transforming
Mission Driven

John 1:14 *The Word became flesh and blood, and moved into the neighborhood.*
John 15:1-2 *"I am the Real Vine and my Father is the Farmer. He cuts off every branch of me that doesn't bear grapes. And every branch that is grape-bearing he prunes back so it will bear even more it in order to bring forth new growth.*

CHAPTER 13

THE LETHBRIDGE ALBERTA BRIDGE
CANADIAN MINISTRY

Be alert, be present.
I'm about to do something brand-new.
It's bursting out! Don't you see it?

Isaiah 43:19

The great 'fly-over' area of North America is where you find the simple life. Yet even this much maligned part of the continent is subject to the corrosive influence of the Broadway-Hollywood media axis. I believe that this is why God chose to raise up one of His great media ministries in an out of the way place like Lethbridge, Alberta, Canada! Did you catch the name? Lethbridge has become one of the crucial bridges in our life and ministry.

We were first introduced to the place over 14 years ago, back in 1994 by our old friend Jerry Wolcson. He and his wife Teresa took us along with them to a conference at the Victory Church in Lethbridge. It was there that we met Pastor Dick and Joan Dewert, the hosts of the conference. Jerry and Teresa Wolcson have been our friends for over 25 years. They were driving through Memphis on their way to a conference in East Tennessee when they heard our program, 'A Drink From the Rock' on a Christian radio station. When they arrived at the conference they overheard our voices and recognized that we were the ones they had just heard on the radio.

Radio is an effective tool for getting your name and that of your ministry out to the public and in achieving voice recognition. We were on the air with radio for about 6 years and during that time and for years after we were amazed at the number of people who would recognize our voices. We've had people come up to us in grocery stores, malls, and other public venues and ask if we were Fred and Val.

Our format was a 15 minute teaching program but there are other ways to go. Radio and TV can be effective bridge builders to a community whether you are in a startup work, as we were, or in a large successful church and desire to expand your sphere of influence.

In 1994 Jerry and Teresa Wolcson told us that they were on their way to a conference in Alberta, Canada. As we had never been to Western Canada and enjoyed their company, we invited ourselves along for the ride. It was one of those spontaneous things that often happen amongst friends. We didn't go to minister, just to see the other side of Val's country and spend some time with our friends.

We arrived at the Victory Church in Lethbridge, Alberta during their summer Camp Meeting. It was a great church of nearly a 1,000 people and we thoroughly enjoyed the meetings. Toward the end of the week the pastor asked me to minister at a leadership luncheon which was part of the conference. He was impressed with what I shared and decided to lengthen the conference by one day and give me a chance to minister to the entire congregation.

It was the beginning of a great ministry relationship with him and we were privileged to minister in his church on several occasions over the years. Just as Jerry was a bridge for us to Western Canada, he was a bridge for us to a wonderful network of churches called Victory Churches International and ultimately to the Miracle Channel. The Miracle Channel would become our bridge to Canada and the world! I'll delve into that more later, but right now I want to share more about the role of relationships as bridges.

The primary reason I have favor in Canada is my precious wife Valerie. What began over 40 years ago in snowy New Brunswick blossomed into a marriage and family that has blessed me beyond measure. Every good thing in my life has come from God through my lifelong mate Valerie. I am a Christian, a minister of the Gospel, a father, a grandfather and a Global television host because of this woman from the Maritimes in Canada. Who could have imagined what would become of Fred & Val and their offspring a generation ago? When I met Valerie I was a troubled young man but she has faithfully been my bridge over troubled waters.

Throughout the nineties and into the 21st century we ministered with Victory Churches International. We ministered in their churches, their conferences, and received their ministers into our church in Memphis. It was a privilege for us to serve as their USA representative for a number of years but then things came to an end. There are times and seasons for all things and apparently our involvement in Victory Churches had come to an end.

Drs. George and Hazel Hill have been pioneers of a truly great work that has spread across the globe. George is from the UK and Hazel is from Australia. Like us their marriage is a bridge between two great countries. After all their success in Canada they relocated to California and started afresh. We bless them and honor them for advancing the kingdom of God on earth in such a powerful way.

In the mid-nineties I sent my son Chris to a Youth Conference at the Victory Church. When he came back I called him into my office for a debriefing. He began to rave about this godly man who received him into his house and his beautiful daughters. I told him that I didn't send him to Canada to meet girls, but I couldn't have been more mistaken. Once again the Lord brought a Memphis boy into relationship with a Canadian girl who would change his life and continue the bridge between our family and the USA and Canada. Chris would go on to marry Becky Mediwake from the Victory Church in Lethbridge, Alberta. I think you can see why we believe that God is doing something in our family to build a bridge between Canada and the USA.

Relationships are so powerful and that is especially true of family. We have been privileged to travel to Mervyn Mediwake's home country of Sri Lanka on several occasions. Muriel is a Scottish lass that Mervyn met while attending University in England. They eventually immigrated to Canada where Mervyn became a successful agri-businessman and Muriel a real estate broker. They reared three beautiful daughters, Naomi, Anne Marie and Becky who is married to our son Chris.

Mervyn and Muriel Mediwake moved to Memphis in 2005 to help us weather the storms of transition as we prepared to turn the work of our lives, Christ The Rock Church over to Chris and Becky. The Mediwakes are not only family but invaluable friends and ministers of the gospel. We thought Memphis was their final destination but God had other plans. After about 2 years in Memphis we learned that their second daughter Anne Marie and her husband Daryl were to be blessed with triplets! This was a confirming sign to a word the Lord had given us in prayer that 2007 would be a year of multiples! What we didn't understand was their return to Canada. Had we missed God? Was it not his will for them to leave Lethbridge and move to Memphis? Why were they moving to Toronto?

When Mervyn and Muriel moved to Memphis it bridged the gap between us and Dick Dewert. We invited him to a Winter Conference and he in turn invited us to make a guest appearance on their Partner Week for the Miracle Channel. Although we had some television experience in Memphis, it was nothing like Partner Week. We had taken our radio program 'A Drink From the Rock' to television. We were forced off the air when an evangelical group bought the station we were on. They objected to a woman, Val, teaching on the air and to our openness about the things of the Spirit.

God will shut you down in one area in order to take you to something higher and better. The loss of our radio program was the impetus to start our own television program but that was not the end of it either. It was really just part of the process. We taped our own program and also served TBN as hosts of their local broadcast in Memphis. In all of these efforts God was working for our good, preparing us for the day when we would be guests and later hosts of the Miracle Channel. God was building another bridge in our lives. At the age of 61! None of our past experiences are for naught. Our history dictates our destiny. The lives we live with all of its experiences good or bad will be used by God to propel us into our future.

CHAPTER 14

THE TRANSFER BRIDGE
HOPE PRESBYTERIAN CHURCH

Why are you downcast, O my soul? Put your hope in
God, for I will yet praise him, my Savior and my God.

Psalms 42:5

Driving down busy Walnut Grove Road in Memphis I was reading the church signs. Memphis is a city of churches so there are plenty of these signs to read. Some of them are funny, some are profound and some are just pathetic. As I passed Hope Presbyterian Church, I saw a banner advertising their 'seven' Christmas Eve services. For the next block I was pondering why any church needed 7 Christmas Eve services and decided to turn around and go back and ask. The receptionist told me that they needed 7 services because over 10,000 people were coming! Now they had my attention. When Val and I had last visited Hope nearly 10 years before they were of comparable size with Christ the Rock and worshipping in a similar multipurpose facility. I was shocked to learn they had grown to such an enormous size. After all, they were Presbyterians, people we derisively called God's 'frozen chosen'! How could or would God be moving in the midst of people so spiritually cold?

In January of that year I was determined to find out what was going on and I began attending a pastors' lunch that Hope's senior pastor Dr. Craig Strickland hosted at the church. The first thing I noticed was that it was a very eclectic bunch of pastors and leaders from various churches, denominations and races. I must admit to a bit of jealousy as I saw many pastors from my own charismatic stream in attendance who had never or rarely attended any of our conferences and pastors' lunches at Christ the Rock. I couldn't understand why they were attending these meetings and what they hoped to get from it. I soon realized that this Church Developers' Network was not something to be suspicious of, or feared and resented. It was really a bridge to the wider body of Christ in Memphis.

The Church Developers' Network had started with

a small group of new church planters who gathered to Craig Strickland for consultation on how to plant and grow successful churches. Their churches were variously Latino, African-American, Disciples of Christ, Methodist, Charismatic, and in the case of Hope, Evangelical Presbyterian. I found that it was very liberating to walk across this bridge so that I could witness what God was doing with those outside my own stream. Other such efforts in Memphis had always been very limited in scope and rarely had a well defined purpose. Mostly the other meetings were about making a few announcements and eating lunch. But this was different as the purpose of the CDN was to grow churches, all kinds of churches, without regard to their theology or culture.

From the outset there were those who questioned or were downright hostile to my crossing this bridge. The senior staff at our church was disdainful of my growing involvement with the CDN and particularly the new ideas and strategies I sought to introduce to them. Some of my charismatic pastor friends visited but saw no benefit in what we were doing. I really had no idea what the cost and the benefits would ultimately be but I felt compelled to cross over the bridge. Many said that I was becoming Presbyterian which seemed totally absurd to me. I wonder if some of Craig Strickland's friends were concerned that I might turn him into a charismatic.

A house at the end of the cove where we live in Memphis, just two doors down from ours, was rented a few years ago. It is quite unusual for a house in our neighborhood to be rented so we were quite curious to see who the new temporary neighbors might be. Since gardening is one of my hobbies I am often out in the yard. At first many of our neighbors thought I was a gardener hired by a homeowner because they saw me outside so often. One day as I was working away in the front garden I heard the garage door on the newly rented house open and thought; now I'll get a chance to see who has moved in. A steel blue BMW Z3 came roaring out of the garage into the street and stopped right in front of where I was working. I could hardly believe my eyes! The driver was Dr. Craig Strickland, senior pastor of Hope Presbyterian Church, of all people. Over the next several months he would often wave or stop and chat for a moment on his way out.

I had asked Craig on a couple of occasions if he would meet me for a cup of coffee. He always said, 'Sure!' but never followed through on my invitation. I just assumed he was too busy or just not interested in our relationship going past the superficial level. Over a year went by and one day I received a phone call at my office from Craig asking me to meet him for lunch. I was floored and wondered what had prompted this sudden change of heart. We met at 'Yia Yia's', a restaurant in Germantown. After exchanging pleasantries he looked across the table at me and said, "I need to ask for your forgiveness." I said, "For what?" He said, "For not following through on your invitations to meet for coffee." I must confess that I was surprised. It is highly unusual for pastors to relate to one another on such an intimate and spiritual level. And that is especially true of the pastors of large churches.

I was more than happy to forgive Craig and amazed that the pastor of a very large Presbyterian church would go to such lengths. It was the only time I remember anything like it happening in over 30 years of ministry. Craig indicated that he wanted to get to know me better and see where we might work together. I don't know if I was being mischievous and testing his sincerity but I asked him to consider going with Val and I to Zambia the next month. I really didn't expect him to say yes, and he didn't. He began to back pedal and offer the excuse that he was about to leave on a sabbatical to Spain. Not knowing what that was all about I let him off the hook and we parted amicably.

By the time I got back to my office I had a telephone call from Craig's administrative assistant, Bob Russell. He wanted to know what I had said to Craig and where was Zambia. Craig must have realized that I was testing our new relationship and decided to follow through. I was once again astounded by this man and his willingness to build bridges.

We've been ministering in Zambia for several years with our friend Dr. Nevers Mumba and his network of Victory Churches. On this particular trip we would be leading a conference in the capital of Lusaka for church leaders. In an amazing turn of events, Nevers had been appointed, not elected, Vice President of the nation by the President of Zambia. This of course lent tremendous weight to our efforts and the impact was not lost on Craig Strickland. Almost every night the Vice President's motorcade would arrive at the conference venue and we would cue up to form a receiving line. Craig got a big kick out of this and it certainly made our efforts look good.

The meetings were thoroughly Pentecostal and I don't know if Craig had ever been involved in anything like them before. But what a trooper he was, teaching on his specialty of 'church growth' in workshops to overflow crowds hungry for what he was sharing, and preaching in the big meeting on two nights. He was right in the midst of it all seemingly without reservations. He was with us when we prayed for people and witnessed all that accompany such meetings.

One morning I told Craig that a group of mission's minded people from Christ the Rock were traveling to the village of Sompani in the Gwimbe Valley. He was very keen to know what we were doing there and told his missions director to go along on the trip. Sompani was one of the villages where Christ the Rock Church had installed a hammer mill for grinding corn. The hammer mills cost about $3,500 at the time but the impact on the local economy was amazing.

We traveled for five hours in a 4 by 4, 2 hours on road and the balance cross country. It was the roughest ride of my life and I quickly learned what the handle above the door was for. It was to keep you from being thrown out the window! When we finally arrived at the village we parked at the foot of a steep hill and proceeded on foot. I noticed a hole in a dry river bed which is their only source of water. It was covered in green slime and two cows were drinking from it. They had to hand carry enough water for their village up that hill every day that it did not rain. As we climbed the hill we began to hear a noise and then we saw them coming out to meet us in precession. It was one of the most humbling experiences I've ever had. I felt more than a little embarrassed at the reception because I knew it wasn't about me. It was about the love of God working through His people, the Body of Christ on earth, to touch the lives of people in a far away and desperate place.

It was one of those times where you feel like the donkey's colt Jesus rode into Jerusalem. You know the applause is not for you! And this was later confirmed when the village elders presented me with a list of things they wanted us to do. It included everything from building a road to their isolated village, to electrifying their homes! That simple hammer mill which operates on a 2 cycle engine had given them hope for so much more. It is the kind of economic empowerment that can change lives and give people hope for the future. The 2,000 people who lived in the village of Sompani had been destitute but now they were a little less so.

For whatever reasons, Craig's missions' director decided not to go. Craig was furious. It wouldn't be long before that man was dismissed. You see, many, maybe most, people are not bridge crossers because they don't want to change or maybe they just can't see the bridge. Craig and I had built the bridge and by faith we could see it! Others must be desperate enough to crossover.

I'm reminded of the scene in the Indiana Jones movie, "The Last Crusade" where Indy is standing on the edge of a chasm and needs to cross over to the other side. It is a matter of life and death as Indy's father's life depends on him finding the Holy Grail and giving his father a drink from it. In desperation he steps out into seemingly thin air and discovers that there is a bridge he could not see from where he had been standing. Perhaps it is a matter of motivation. Are you desperate enough to risk all in order to crossover?

There are several ways to approach missions. Traditionally, the church has sent missionaries to foreign lands where they would live and die sowing their life for the sake of the Gospel. In modern times as transportation and communication improved missionaries we able to periodically go home on furlough before returning to their mission field. In my capacity as senior pastor at Christ the Rock Church, I would travel abroad on short term missions' trips several times a year. Over the last 25 years I have been privileged to travel to 5 continents and in 35 nations while flying over 3 million miles. As more and more nations have been influenced by the Gospel and indigenous churches and ministries have sprung up, it was my goal to work with these national ministries. The strategy was to promote and develop indigenous with conferences and to give them money that had previously gone to Western missionaries.

Today we see another shift taking place in missions as churches are committing to send as many of their members as possible on short term missions trips. We witness a great deal of this kind of ministry wherever there has been a natural disaster. Christ the Rock along with many other churches sent teams into the hurricane affected areas of the Gulf basin, scores of church lay-people flew into the affected areas.

Mervyn Mediwake and I were in Sri Lanka a week before the tsunami struck. We had been ministering in a conference high in the mountains and later in some churches on the northern shore in the city of Jaffna. When the news of the catastrophe reached us we began to pray about what we could do. I went to my friend Pastor Craig Strickland and told him that if any of the churches in the Church Developers' Network wanted to help, we had a small group of churches in Sri Lanka who could facilitate them. Craig called a week later and asked me to meet him at the Starbuck's in Cordova. When I arrived he handed me a check. He had gone before his great congregation and received an offering for the churches in Sri Lanka. The check was for more than $100,000! I was floored! I had never witnessed such a generous act in which a denominational church would sow a missions' offering of this size into a non-denominational church.

I gave the check to Mervyn and he returned to his homeland of Sri Lanka and organized the relief and rebuilding effort for his network of churches. Although Christians are a small and often persecuted minority in Sri Lanka which is overwhelmingly Buddhist, the Christians were the first ones on the scene of the disaster to offer aid and comfort. Some of the Hope investment went into immediate relief so that people could eat. In the affected villages along the coast, nearly everything necessary to sustain daily life had been swept out to sea. The people were homeless, without fresh water, and they had nothing to eat and little to wear except the clothes on their backs. Emergency survival kits were purchased and distributed in the short-term. And then Mervyn organized the building of a village that was named Hope. Because the Christians had helped everyone regardless of their religious faith, the local government did the same when it came to the allocation of the housing. Hope village stands as a testimony today to the faith and missionary zeal of two churches in faraway Memphis, Tennessee. But it also stands as a testimony of collaboration with the indigenous Sri Lankan church. Since that day the churches have been growing and the people of Sri Lanka, especially in the devastated areas have looked upon Christians with great favor.

This missions' trip to Zambia was the beginning of ongoing collaboration between Craig Strickland at Hope Church in Memphis, and our family. Craig has been a mentor to our son Chris who is now the senior pastor of Christ the Rock Church. Our son-in-law Jeremy Horn had an album produced by Hope's recording label, 'The Grove'. And I have served the Church Developers' Network Craig founded for two years. Recently I became the Missions Director at Hope Church. What an adjustment this has been after 30 years as a senior pastor! And yet I don't view it as the end but as a bridge to something new that the Lord has for me.

Hope is a very different church culture from Christ the Rock Church and reminds me of the Methodist Church where I started in ministry over 30 years ago. It has been helpful for me to see how a larger than Christ the Rock Church operates. I've discovered that Hope is going through some fo the same stresses that Christ the Rock experienced after building a large sanctuary. The big difference is that they have managed to continue growing. Nevertheless, they have been forced to make some painful changes. Craig has curtailed his missions travel and is focused on growing the church and increasing giving.

Hope built a 5,000 seat sanctuary that opened a little over a year ago. Based on projections from past performance they expected a 20% growth rate. Now I know that figure seems excessive but they had done it before and filled up everything they had built. Even today, Hope is offering four services a weekend, one on Saturday night and three on Sunday morning. That is over 6,500 adults in attendance every weekend. These kinds of numbers put Hope into the top 100 churches in America. And yet it has been an uphill struggle to meet the financial obligations of their mortgage.

It will be interesting to see what will happen in the midst of the economic downturn that has struck the world. Hope has restructured their loan with the bank.

They have shed staff though attrition and some lay-offs. They have changed their fiscal year for budget purposes by stretching out the year by four months. They have focused on donor development by showing extra attention and special gratitude to the bigger givers in the church. One new employee has been hired to work on donor development. Department heads are required to submit monthly reports showing how they are helping by growing their departments. Everything is focused on growing the church.

There are still places in the world where the best strategy is to send missionaries who are called and willing to move to a foreign land and invest their lives and ministry for the sake of the Gospel. They are the pioneers who deserve the support of the church as they plow and break new ground for the kingdom of God! There are many other places where the labor of lifelong missionaries has sprung forth in vibrant indigenous churches. The best way to nurture these works is by sending skilled and anointed ministers to train and equip their ministers for greater growth. And there are some places in the world where the people are so poor and conditions so desperate that anyone who calls on the name of Christ can go and be a blessing. This is where the typical church member can have a missions' experience that may be life changing for them. These three strategies are not mutually exclusive and they often overlap.

There are different strategies for church growth both at home and abroad. They all overlap and grow out of one another. Some of the DNA of the last move of God will continue on in the next. Rather than being jealous or suspicious we should embrace the new things God is doing to grow His church. This is what Building Bridges

Together is all about. Building Bridges between nations, generations, cultures, churches and various moves of God so that His kingdom may come and His will be done on this earth as it is in heaven!

Amos 9:13 NIV *"The days are coming," declares the Lord, "when the reaper will be overtaken by the plowman and the planter by the one treading grapes.*

CHAPTER 15

THE MEDIA BRIDGE
FORTY YEARS LATER

He brought me out into a spacious place;
he rescued me because he delighted in me.

Psalms 18:19 NIV

The Dewerts were wonderful hosts of the Miracle Channel. I was amazed by how they managed the six hours of live programming each night of the week during their telethons. Money had to be raised through partners that supported the only twenty-four hour Christian Television network because the station is not allowed to sell commercial time. The call letters are CJIL which stands for Christ Jesus Is Lord! The former hosts and several others gave everything they had to establish and build the Miracle Channel. After 12 years in which they led over 70 partner weeks and taped countless other programs they resigned and left the ministry. We were shocked by the sudden end to their leadership at the Miracle Channel. But however it happens and for whatever reason, I believe that it is all part of something bigger than any person or ministry. Over the last few years we have witnessed a wave of change in ministries as one generation and style of leadership has given way to another.

There have been several prophesies about a new generation of leaders rising up and taking their positions in the kingdom of God. They are largely people who are unknown or hidden. They are like the prophets who were hidden in a cave in Elijah's day. Elijah thought he was the last of the prophets but the Lord reminded him that Obadiah had hidden 100 prophets of God from the murderous Jezebel in two caves and was sustaining them with food and water until the Lord needed them and called them forth.
(I Kings 18:4)

For some time I have wondered about the numbers of Spirit filled people who have remained in or returned to churches and ministries that were not Charismatic or Pentecostal. Could it be they are hidden from the murderous spirit of Jezebel who has brought so many down? I believe that this is also part of God's next great move. We have been blessed by the modern Pentecostal movement and even more by the Charismatic movement of the last 40 years but now it is time for something new. Whatever God does, He does from glory to glory to ever greater glory. Old things are passing away and behold the Lord is doing a new thing. Prophet James Goll says that every new move of God has a new sound, a new manifestation and a new revelation.

Moses was hidden in the wilderness until that day God appeared to him in a burning bush and called him out for the great work he was to do in leading Israel out of Egyptian bondage. David was hidden in the cave of Adullam from the murderous Saul who sought to kill God's true anointed king. Jesus was hidden from Herod, first in Egypt and later in the obscurity of Nazareth until the appointed time when He would come forth and lead all of humanity out of the darkness and into the light of God's kingdom. These and other pivotal figures were hidden, humble and hated injustice. These are the marks of the new kingdom generation who are coming forth even now!

What about us? What about our generation? Most will not cross over into this new kingdom day but there are some like Joshua and Caleb who will be used of God to help this new generation. Joshua and Caleb survived the 40 years of wilderness wandering because they were the faithful ones who had been ready to go into the Promised Land the first time. They were men of a different spirit. There are some like Obadiah who will hide and provide for the true prophets of God who have not worshipped the gods of the land. Val and I want to be like them. We want to enter into all that God has promised and help others to enter in. Rather than thinking we are the only ones left, we want to go to those who are in the caves hidden and help to bring them, spring them, send them into their glorious destiny.

It was May of 2008 when Mervyn Mediwake called and asked if we could come to Lethbridge, Alberta and host the Partner Week which is the telethon to raise funds because Christian television has no commercial ads to sponsor it except through the donations of supporters. As the new chairman of the board he was determined to turn things around at the Miracle Channel but everyone he asked to come and help refused or excused themselves. Val and I were his last choice and possibly his last chance. Truly, many are called but few are chosen. I was on my way to Zambia in Central Africa but told him that we would pray about it and give him an answer as soon as possible. The Lord spoke to us that very evening and I called him back the next morning to tell him that we would do it. We had already raised the money for the African conference and our dear friend Colin Carson from Manchester, England very graciously released me from my commitment. He went alone and the Lord used him mightily in ministering to the leaders in Zambia.

What was so strange is that a year prior to this invitation to host, the Lord had put the burden of the Miracle Channel in our hearts. We did not understand why, except maybe to pray and stand with the people while they were going through this extremely difficult transition. This ministry is without a shadow of doubt God's ministry. He birthed it just like He birthed Jesus through Mary. He was God's ministry to the world never Mary's. We had been guests on several partner weeks but had never hosted one before. It was a real step of faith for us as we tried to remember and emulate the best we could what we had seen previous hosts do. There is something so sovereign about sitting down in a positional seat of authority and sensing the anointing of the Lord like never before. The Spirit of the Lord came upon us and we found ourselves being used of God in a completely new way.

We were then asked to host the Dominion Conference in June of 2008 and once again the Lord stepped up big for us. God had prepared us to host because we had had the privilege of hosting numerous great conferences at our church in Memphis with wonderful national and international speakers. Val and I both ministered like we never had before. It was such a blessing to serve the Miracle Channel. We believe this ministry has changed the atmosphere of Canada. We believe God raised it up to position Canada to reach the nations of the world.

After the conference, we were asked to host the flag ship show entitled 'The Bridge' which was going to begin taping in September to debut in October. We were in absolute awe at what God was doing. Who are we to be the hosts of the Miracle Channel! Who would have thought, two insignificant individuals, one from New Brunswick and the other from Tennessee, would be hosting the Miracle Channel! God has a great sense of humor! We are now on a new learning curve. We feel we are riding a wave and don't know where it is going. We realized God had been preparing us all these years for such a time as this.

Like Esther of old, we felt we were brought to the kingdom for such a time as this. What was even more exciting was the fact that Val, would be ministering to her fellow Canadians which is a dream come true. She has been ministering in the US for well over thirty years and she would love to give the rest of her life serving Canada. So we committed to coming up once a month to tape twenty or more shows. Who would have thought! God was ordering our steps. When we gave up our program in Memphis in 2006, we thought that was the end of our media days. We had to die to that ministry which we did. We have always enjoyed television ministry and had felt called to it. The feedback we received was always positive. Still we had to die to it so that He would resurrect it in His timing. The gifts and callings are irrevocable.

Then we remembered what Ray Block, the former CEO of the Miracle Channel and an intercessor told us in the fall of 2007, a year prior to us becoming leaders of the Miracle Channel. He had told us while in prayer that he had had a vision of us sitting in the pilot seats of a jet and he likened that to the seats of leadership of the Miracle Channel. We were blown away so to speak! However, that very morning Fred and I awakened with the burden of the channel in our hearts. It was very heavy and we had no idea what it meant except maybe to pray. We knew it was God so like Mary, we just pondered this thing in our hearts. Another couple had been leading the ministry since the beginning of 2007. Through a series of events, the ministry sort of fell in our laps and here we are sitting in the pilot seats. And we are experiencing the ride of a lifetime! Who would have thought - at this time in our lives!

We returned home after the conference and our church had a grand celebration in July to honor us for 25 years of service to Christ the Rock Church which we founded, 30 years of pastoring and our 40th wedding anniversary. They blessed Val with a brand new polar white SAAB. It is one of the most unexpected blessings we have ever received, although Val, who has given several cars to others over the years, had been in faith for one. She calls it her polar bear! The church has also provided me with a leased car as part of my retirement from Christ The Rock.

July 24th, 2008 we departed Memphis in Val's new car. We were going to a family reunion in Montreal Canada. The drive from Memphis northward was pleasant and blessed. We have always enjoyed driving distances together. Somehow it is restful and gives us a chance to unplug from all our responsibilities and 're-center'. Traffic was manageable; Kroger gas was affordable; and the Hampton Inn was restful.

On July 25th, we crossed the Ambassador Bridge between Detroit, Michigan and Windsor, Ontario. Once again there was a real sense that what we had not been able to do in 1968 when we were married was now coming to pass. It was our desire to live in Canada! Is it possible that 40 years later the Lord is calling us back to Canada?

Upon our arrival in the Greater Toronto Area, GTA as the media call it, we stayed with Mervyn and Muriel Mediwake. These dear friends are so symbolic of what we have been about for the past 40 years. They have been greatly used of God to position us for what He is doing now and for what lies ahead.

We first met the Mediwakes in 1994 during a visit to Lethbridge, Alberta, Canada when we tagged along with our old friends, the Wolcsons. Mervyn's testimony on how he was groomed to be a Buddhist monk but converted to Christianity in Canada is miraculous. It is recorded in 'Voice', a publication of the Full gospel Business men's Fellowship - issue 41, number 8, August 1993.

While in Toronto, the four of us met with George Woodward who was the partner relations representative for the Miracle Channel in Ontario at that time. His wife, Marilyn, had an inspiration to take us to a camp meeting in Copetown, Ontario with Russ and Mave Moyer whom we had never met. They were having prophetic meetings from Canada Day (July 1) until Labor Day (first Monday of Sept). The Moyers conduct continuous meetings in a tent. Russ Moyer had a prophecy for us which confirmed the call of God where the Miracle Channel is concerned.

And I quote the gist from a transcript of the tape he gave us: "I see you as a strong stabilizing force. I see you having gone through two very difficult and dark seasons close together. And your hearts were broken for the people around you. You had some broken hearted experiences and God's kind of brought you back together and brought some pieces of the puzzle back together. But some people made some bad choices and bad decisions and you had to pay a price for that and you got caught up in the whole vicious cycle of what happened. And there was a cycling that had to happen and now I see it cycling out and now I'm going to flush some things out. And He says as I finish the flushing out process there is going to be something that clears the way for you. And now I look and all of a sudden there are fish in the water.

And the Lord says, 'I'm going to set you in a place, a supernatural place and the supernatural is going to be natural, but you're going to have the ability to believe for the miraculous, that miracles are going to come and they're going to come in abundance.' And the lord says, 'You're going to believe for the great harvest, even the great harvest that has been behind you, but a great harvest that is still yet to come.' Your greatest days are yet to come. I see you going down the road. Lots of people of influence! I see you with a ministry of compassion. I see you with a ministry of helps. But I see you also with a ministry of leadership and ability and decision making. I see you standing as faithful pillars. I see you having learned from some things that occurred.

You're very strong and you're very mature in your gifting and your calling. There is great leadership and I see a spotlight coming on. The light was dark and somebody flipped the switch on and a platform expanded and enlarged and now the curtain is pulled back. Now the platform is moving out to the front and the lights are coming. Three very important things needed to happen. Don't retreat any longer! Don't even think about occupying, now is an invasion time! It's a pursuing time, it's time to recapture everything that was taken, everything that was stolen. Hallelujah!"

This word confirmed what had transpired. The two difficult seasons were the transition in our church and that of the Miracle Channel. The platform was the new television program we are hosting, 'The Bridge'. God truly gave us the courage to pursue His will where the Miracle Channel is concerned. We knew God would work out the details. It seemed very complicated with us living in Memphis and the Channel being in Lethbridge. Then there was the ministry at Christ the Rock and Hope Churches in Memphis, and finally, Fred being a US citizen and me holding dual citizenship: Canada and US. But with God, all things are possible. It truly is a walk of faith. We are surfing the waves. It sure beats being surrounded by the shakings we have gone through.

We did not strive to make any of this happen. In fact we were not even the first choice to be the hosts. But I have to believe we were God's choice because of all the prophetic words we received confirming what God was doing. It seemed like everyone had abandoned ship when the shaking began. We experienced a similar reaction in our church when we passed the reins of leadership to our son. No one likes change because it disrupts equilibrium and they would rather just remain comfortable or jump ship and leave. Change is almost a curse word. God knows what He is doing and is always working behind the scenes because destiny is on His mind. We can trust that whatever He does on our behalf is good and He will get the glory.

Jeremiah 29:11 *I know what I'm doing. I have it all planned out — plans to take care of you, not abandon you, plans to give you the future you hope for.* We just kept praying and minding our own business. I am reminded of
1 Peter 5:5-6 *"God opposes the proud but gives grace to the humble." Humble yourselves, therefore, under God's mighty hand, that he may lift you up in due time.*

CONCLUSION

So, go now and write all this down.
Put it in a book
So that the record will be there
to instruct the coming generations,

Isa 30:8

Last winter, 2008, Val and I were traveling to Lethbridge, Alberta for a time of ministry at the Miracle Channel. We have often used these trips to Canada as an opportunity to go skiing so we were wearing and lugging some of our ski equipment. After checking in at the Memphis airport and spending a little preflight time in the Northwest Airlines World Club we began walking to the gate for our flight. I noticed that it felt like I had accidentally stepped into something so I stopped to clean off what I suspected was a wad of gum on the heal of my snow boot. Much to my surprise I discovered that the heel of my boot was falling apart. Not just falling off, but actually disintegrating! Since we were already halfway to the gate and our bags with my other shoes were checked there wasn't anything I could do but limp on over to the departure gate and board the plane.

Upon our flight's arrival in Minneapolis, the scene of the bridge collapse, we had to walk some distance to the next gate for our flight to Calgary. I now noticed that both my boots were feeling funny. Once again I stopped to investigate and discovered that the heel of the other boot was also disintegrating and I was leaving a trail of shoe debris behind me. Fortunately, I was able to find a shoe store in the airport mall and purchase a new pair of boots.

I've never had anything like this happen before and it really arrested my attention. And the more I thought about this unlikely occurrence the more I felt like it had some significance. The Spirit of the Lord began to minister to me as I asked, "What's up with this?" I was reminded that while the Children of Israel were in the wilderness neither their clothes nor their shoes wore out. We certainly knew what the wilderness felt like! But now the Lord was introducing us to something new. We were "crossing over" into something new.

Deut. 29:5 NIV says, *"During the forty years that I led you through the desert, your clothes did not wear out, nor did the sandals on your feet."*

I sensed the Spirit asking me, "What do you think happened, what changed when they stepped into the Promised Land?" As I pondered this in light of what I had just experienced with my old boots, it struck me that their shoes may well have begun to deteriorate because they had crossed over into something new. The Scripture doesn't declare it but it is implied in the stoppage of other wilderness provision. Consider some of the following scriptures:

Exodus 16:35 NIV *"The Israelites ate manna forty years, until they came to a land that was settled; they ate manna until they reached the border of Canaan."*

Joshua 5:11-12 *NIV "The day after the Passover, that very day, they ate some of the produce of the land: unleavened bread and roasted grain. The manna stopped the day after they ate this food from the land; there was no longer any manna for the Israelites, but that year they ate the produce of Canaan."*

Nehemiah 9:25 NIV *"They ate to the full and were well-nourished; they reveled in your great goodness."*

On this trip, we were crossing over into our Promised Land. Over the last year Canada and the Miracle Channel have certainly proven to be our Promised Land! God had been preparing us all along. We never go through anything without there being a purpose. For us, giving up the local church propelled us to become the hosts of 'The Bridge', the flagship program of the Miracle Channel, the only 24/7 Canadian Christian Network. Praise God! This media is changing the climate of Canada and we praise Him for allowing us to be a part of His plan.

LaVergne, TN USA
05 November 2009

163229LV00004B/13/P